THE FANTASTIC 42: A FELLOWSHIP FACING DOOM WITH HOPE

Eric Anderson
Nathan Marchand
Darrin Ball
Nick Hayden
Chris Cooke
Becky Smith
Scott Bayles

Interior Design by Nathan Marchand
Cover and Artwork by Ruth Pike-Miller
Cover arranged by Bryan Donihue

First Printing

To all the pastors who work tirelessly for their congregations and their communities.

TABLE OF CONTENTS

FOREWORD
BY DALLAS MORA

Years ago in my Bible college days, I had the opportunity to sit in on a class specifically about missions. The instructor brought up an interesting conversation about the issue of *langue*. Not "language," as in translating Greek into Hebrew, but how the mindset attached to a word can vary from people group to people group within the same language group. To illustrate this, he shared the example of an inner-city ministry that found itself struggling to help troubled teens understand the love of God the Father. For them, a father was absent, abusive, and corrupt. Why would they want the love from anyone who was a father? After some time of study and work with these young men, they realized that for many of these young people, the only person ever to exhibit the traits of a true father was their parole officer. So, when they described God, they used the terminology and example of a parole officer from that point on. This marked a massive shift in their ministry as these young people began to genuinely accept the Gospel because, finally, someone spoke in a language they could understand.

Using cultural and regional examples to explain the truths of God is not a new tactic. Paul did this with the Romans. Jesus used this often throughout the Synoptic Gospels. Why? Because the human experience is varied, and while there is a singular truth to the Gospel, everyone comes to it with their worldview and life experiences. Anyone who shares the Gospel must navigate these things to help the hearers to understand it in its Biblical and historical context. Sometimes that means leaning into the hearer's cultural background to bring them to Biblical truth.

In your hands is a book that strives to do that. Nathan, Eric, and the other outstanding contributors came to this book with a particular mission: share the saving truth of Jesus Christ in a manner that geeks, nerds, otakus, and everyone in between can understand. This project was a labor of love; the love for our Lord and Savior, Jesus the Christ, and a love for you, dear reader. Each devotional you'll read was carefully crafted by individuals who "get it." They understand Geek Culture. They love anime, comics, video games, and sci-fi just as much as you do. As you go through these devotionals, please keep this in mind. Understand that their love for you is a true reflection of the love of the Father (or Parole Officer, if you will) for you.

Stay Devoted – Peace and Love
Dallas Mora
Co-Founder of Geek Devotions

DAY 1 - KLAATU'S MISSION
BY ERIC ANDERSON

Since we live by the Spirit, let us keep in step with the Spirit.

Galatians 5:25

The 1951 sci-fi classic *The Day the Earth Stood Still* begins with a flying saucer traveling around the planet before landing in Washington, D.C. just a short walk from the White House. After it has sat there for a time and the army has surrounded it, Klaatu (played by Michael Rennie) walks out of the ship on the suddenly formed ramp and tries to introduce himself peacefully. *Bam!* An item in his hand is dropped after a spooked infantryman fires his pistol. A robot named Gort responds by destroying the soldiers' weapons with some sort of laser, but Klaatu stops him.

Our new alien friend is taken to Walter Reed Medical Center, where he makes a quick recovery from his injuries due to a salve he has brought along for the journey. While there, he meets a secretary for the President, Mr. Harley, who comes to have a discussion. Klaatu asks for a meeting with leaders from every nation on the planet. The small grievances between nations are meaningless to him, and he doesn't understand why they won't come together. His message is not just for the USA, not just for the United Nations, but for everyone. Mr. Harley does approach the President with the request, but then comes back with letters from many nations, including Britain and the USSR, confirming many disagreements about such a meeting. When accused of being impatient, Klaatu says, "I'm impatient with stupidity." He is astonished that the nations will not work together for this.

It is then that he makes a request to go out, talk to people, and explore this world for himself. He desires to meet ordinary people. Harley puts a hard "no" in place and even has the door locked, which seems to amuse Klaatu, who grins at the silliness of the lock. His escape is off-screen, but you get the idea that locked doors do not a prison make for this man from the stars. He does go out, and he finds a room to rent, saying his name is Carpenter. Over this next act of the film, he befriends those in the house, especially a young boy named Bobby Benson (played by Billy Gray) and his mom, Helen Benson (played by Patricia Neal). He and Bobby go out and see many sights. They stop by the gravesite of Bobby's father in Arlington Cemetery and go see the spaceship. Klaatu even "sells" the kid a couple of diamonds for two dollars. Klaatu takes time to teach the kid about rocket science and arithmetic while trying not to expose himself.

Two-thousand years ago, a man came who was not of this world (John 1:10). He arrived by birth to a virgin on a night when angels, also beings not of this world, announced it to shepherds. His name is Jesus, and He wanted to walk among

3

us, eat with us, and teach us many things. His message was also not just for a select few, but for all who would listen. Some did not want his message to go out into the world. They opposed him with many questions, and He did get "impatient with stupidity." He drew many disciples to Himself and taught them numerous lessons. Sometimes He would comment, "O you of little faith," when they seemed confused or scared. In the Hebrew and Christian traditions, there are varying names of God that all focus on different aspects of Him. One of those is Emmanuel, which means, "God with us."

Klaatu eventually meets a scientist named Barnhardt and helps him solve an equation related to space travel. As they decide to set up a meeting for scientists and thinkers to come hear what he would say, the Professor asks for a sign. Something huge that would not hurt anyone. The next day at noon, everything stops. The Earth stands still, so to speak. Electricity is "neutralized" all over the world. Cars, trains, elevators, even malt machines at restaurants are all affected. This lasts for exactly half-an-hour, prompting major fear and discussion. In a meeting at the Pentagon, it is explained that planes are still flying and hospital equipment is not affected by this phenomena. Before the meeting, the army finds Klaatu and manages to shoot him. Helen, who has been helping him get around the city, takes a message to the robot Gort: "Klaatu berada nikto." The robot recovers the body and puts him in a machine in the spacecraft that revives him. Shocked by this, Helen says:

"You mean he has the power of life and death?"

"No, that power is reserved for the Almighty Spirit," replies Klaatu.

Think about that. The power of life and death is reserved for God. I don't have it. You don't have it. But Jesus does. He is 100% man and 100% God. While on Earth, He often healed the sick, gave sight to the blind, and even raised the dead. He even stopped storms with His voice. Klaatu needs equipment for what he does, but even now Jesus just has the power. In his pivotal moment, He chose to allow himself to go through a painful death on a cross to bring redemption (far more painful than the bullets that Klaatu felt) but then came a moment far more powerful than the Earth standing still: Jesus resurrected from the dead! He beat death itself and now sits at the right hand of God the Father.

After being revived, Klaatu finally gives his message to the scientists and thinkers. He has come because many other planets have chosen to cooperate with a set of rules against aggression, and Earth is invited into that alliance. This won't affect any of the multi-national drama on Earth but would affect how humanity interacts galactically. Gort is one of many robots that act as policemen traveling the universe and keeping aggressors in check. Here is some of what Klaatu says:

"This does not mean giving up any freedom +except the freedom to act irresponsibly.... The result is we live in peace without arms or armies. Secure in the knowledge we are free from aggression and war. Free to pursue more profitable enterprises. We do not pretend to be perfect but we have a system and it works.... Your choice is simple: join us and live in peace, or pursue your present course and face obliteration."

Jesus gave us a lot of teachings to think about. He challenged religious leaders who wanted to add unnecessary rules. He called us deeper in the focus and spirit of the law given in the Old Testament. And He changed our understanding of faith. In Matthew 5-7 and Luke 6, we find the Sermon on the Mount, which gives us directives on personal ethics; ways we can be more profitable for those around us and for ourselves.

Romans 6:22 says, "But now being made free from sin, and become servants to God, ye have your fruit unto holiness, and the end everlasting life" (KJV). The agreement ratified for this group of planets was to free them from war and allow them to "pursue more profitable enterprises." Jesus gives us such a strong offer as well. We are free in Him to be rid of sin, to learn self-control, love, peace, goodness, and so much more.

Quest of the Day

1. Read Galatians 5.

2. What sins are you still not free from?

3. What are you pursuing that is profitable?

4. How can you move from a particular sin to something profitable?

DAY 2 - CHIRRUT IMWE: THE FORCE IS WITH ME, AND I AM ONE WITH THE FORCE
BY NATHAN MARCHAND

You, dear children, are from God and have overcome them, because the one who is in you is greater than the one who is in the world.

1 John 4:4

He looked like a blind beggar on the streets of Jedha to Jyn Erso. A man, she was told, who was once a Guardian of the Whills at the Jedi temple that housed the fabled Kyber crystals that powered lightsabers. He preached about the will of the Force, somehow sensing that Jyn had a crystal in her necklace. "The strongest stars have hearts of Kyber," he told her. Later, after she and her comrades Cassian Andor and the droid K2SO are apprehended by Imperial Stormtroopers, Chirrut wanders toward them tapping the ground with his staff. He ignores the troopers' threats and insults, reciting the mantra of the Guardians:

"The Force is with me,

And I am one with the Force;

And I fear nothing,

Because all is as the Force wills it."

A trooper fires, but Chirrut hears the laser blast, dodges it, and proceeds to dismantle the entire platoon in a scene straight out of a Hong Kong martial arts film. (What else did you expect from Donnie Yen?)

When he and his cohort Baze Malbus, along with Jyn and Cassian, are captured by insurgents, Chirrut repeats his mantra while imprisoned in their dungeon. Baze even remarks that it sounds like a prayer. Chirrut isn't a Jedi, but his belief in the Force is absolute and devout. The implication is that his extraordinary combat skills, despite his blindness, somehow stem from the Force.

His faith is put to the ultimate test during the Battle of Scarif at the end of *Rogue One: A Star Wars Story*. He learns that the master switch on the communications array needs to be activated for the Death Star plans to be transmitted to the Rebels. Repeating his mantra, he walks into the line of fire, laser blasts all around him, but none so much as graze him. He flips the switch, but as the blind warrior turns and smiles at Baze, he is finally hit. With his dying breath, he tells his old friend, "It's okay...it's okay. Look for the Force...and you will always find me."

I was struck by Chirrut when I first saw *Rogue One* because his view of the Force seemed more personal, like it was a living being with which he could commune. This was vastly different from the impersonal, well, force described in previous *Star Wars* films. His heightened perceptions and fighting skills, while probably inspired by the blind Japanese swordsman character Zatoichi, seem very much like that of a biblical judge. Someone like Samson would have the "Spirit of the Lord" come "upon him in power" (Judges 14:6, 19, etc.) and perform incredible feats.

But that isn't what this entry is about.

Chirrut recites a mantra to himself (and others) when faced with hardship. "The Force is with me, and I am one with the Force." It's essentially a prayer. He's reminding himself that he serves something far greater. His faith is absolute. If the Force wills it, it can't be stopped. That's why he can walk into the line of fire without fear. He's not unlike the Confederate Civil War general "Stonewall" Jackson, who would ride recklessly into battle believing that unless it was God's will that he die, nothing would hurt him. Prayer is required to have faith like that. It is communication and communion with God. He isn't a distant and impersonal being. He seeks intimacy with us, which we can have thanks to the work of Jesus. Now when we tremble facing an "impossible" task, we can say to ourselves, "You, dear children, are from God and have overcome them, because the one who is in you is greater than the one who is in the world" (1 John 4:4).

To put it another way: "The Lord is with me, and I am one with the Lord."

Quest of the Day

1. Read Joshua 1.

2. Write a list of challenges you face this week, this month, and this year. Be as specific as possible.

3. Carve out an hour where you can be alone, away from any and all distractions (no phone or anything). Perhaps play some worship music to help you focus. With that list in hand, pray over each one. Repeat 1 John 4:4 to yourself, if you have to. Make this a regular (perhaps weekly) practice.

4. Look into "breath prayers," which involve repeating short prayers like, "Jesus Christ, have mercy on me, a sinner," between intervals of deep breathing. Give it a try this week.

DAY 3 - THE UNMATCHED EVIL OF DR. JEKYLL BY DARRIN BALL

The heart is deceitful above all things and beyond cure. Who
can understand it?
Jeremiah 17:9

This classic tale of good versus evil may not be as you think. If you have not read the original novella titled *The Strange Case of Dr. Jekyll and Mr. Hyde* by Robert Louis Stevenson, I urge you to do it soon. People have this impression that Dr. Henry Jekyll was good and Edward Hyde was evil, but this is not the case. The entire premise for Jekyll creating another identity was that he had inner desires that seemed to be the exact opposite of his honorable and distinguished reputation. He states, "I concealed my pleasures," and, "hid them with an almost morbid sense of shame." His conclusion, more as a philosopher than a medical doctor, is that each man has two natures: one good and one evil.

Jekyll created the tincture for the sole purpose of becoming someone else who could indulge in these degradations and not have them associated with the good name of Dr. Henry Jekyll. His belief that man is of two natures is faulty, though, even by his own admission. He wants the potion to separate his good side from his evil side. After the ebullition subsides, and he drinks it for the first time, he is transformed into a small, deformed, diabolical, evil fiend.

12

Upon transforming back, Jekyll was not completely good but still divided. He writes in his journal, "Hence, although I had now two characters as well as two appearances, one was wholly evil, and the other was still the old Henry Jekyll, that incongruous compound of whose reformation and improvement I had already learned to despair. The movement was thus wholly toward the worse."

The main character of the novella is Gabriel John Utterson, Jekyll's lawyer and close friend. He rarely says anything negative about people, confessing that, "I incline to Cain's heresy. I let my brother go to the devil in his own way." The narrative states that he tends to be the last good influence in the lives of down-going men. This is significant foreshadowing in the first paragraph of the book. He seems to break his own rule, though, and counsels Jekyll against any association with this detestable Mr. Hyde, who seems to have some unexplained leverage over Dr. Jekyll. Utterson believes his old friend is sunshine compared to Hyde.

In the midpoint of the plot (although this is only revealed at the end in his journal), Dr. Jekyll has a conscious choice, to be "surrounded by friends and cherishing honest hope," or to indulge in "leaping impulses and secret pleasures that I had enjoyed in the disguise of Hyde." He attempts to choose the good, but the evil never leaves him. His inner desires eventually overpower him, and he drinks the potion once again. This leads to the murder of an innocent man. Afterward, he thinks he has learned his lesson. He confesses to Utterson that he is completely done with Hyde and assures him that Hyde will never appear again. Perhaps Jekyll thought he was finished with Hyde, but the evil within Henry Jekyll that created Hyde was still there and would continue to torment him.

I hope you don't mind the spoilers. The story is classic, iconic, and universal. We all know that Jekyll and Hyde are the same person. I hope you will read the original tale with this in mind: *Dr. Jekyll may have been brilliant as a doctor, but his moral compass couldn't have pointed further from the truth.* Instead of believing that part of him was good, Jekyll should have turned to God for salvation from his entirely sinful state of being. It wasn't good versus evil; it was the sin of pride (outward appearance) versus the sin of debauchery. The separation that occurred with the drinking of the potion was only a separation of different types of sinfulness. He states in his journal, "The drug had no discriminating action; it was neither diabolical nor divine; it but shook the doors of the prisonhouse of my disposition." Basically, he let out the evil from within.

Scriptural truth is alluded to frequently in this short story:

- "My devil had been long caged, he came out roaring."

- "The Babylonian finger on the wall, to be spelling out the letters of my judgment."

Perhaps the most heartbreaking,

- "Utterson," said the voice, "for God's sake, have mercy!"

Even though truth was near, Jekyll never turned to God. He tried to handle his demons on his own. If he had only believed the Scriptures and how they portray the sinful plight of mankind! The Bible says, "For all have sinned and fall short of the glory of God" (Romans 3:23). Jekyll could have been convicted by this passage: "Their feet rush into sin; they are swift to shed innocent blood. They pursue evil schemes; acts of violence mark their ways" (Isaiah 59:7).

Maybe you don't think this is you. Maybe you think you are a pretty good person. That is not the language of the Bible. The Bible describes all of us as sinful; we just have different sins. Here are a few that you may or may not struggle with: pride, anger, lust, gluttony, drunkenness, gossip, disobeying parents, dirty jokes, lying, sexual immorality (even looking can be a sin), cursing, stealing, bragging, hatred, name calling (even just saying, "You fool"), judging others, violence, impatience, selfishness.

Have you experienced this inner struggle? Have you tried to keep a good outward appearance because you want to be perceived as upright? Do you have desires that you would be ashamed of if certain people found out?

Instead of denying that you are sinful or creating an outlet for your sin like Jekyll did, confess your sins to God. Jesus died on the cross for your sins. His blood was shed in order to purchase you (1 Peter 1:18-19). The Bible says if we deny our sinfulness then we are liars, but if we confess our sins, that God is faithful and just to forgive us from our sins (1 John 1:8-10). Believe this truth: that God loves you and wants you to be forgiven. You must have faith in Jesus Christ because He is the only way to be saved from your sins. Ask for that forgiveness today.

Jimmy Needham, one of my favorite music artists, has a song called "Jekyll & Hyde" on his album *Vice and Virtue*. Here are a few lyrics:

There is a lunatic in everyone I know

Some live it out

Some just refuse to drink the potion, baby

But we're all monsters inside

Cause we act like Dr. Jekyll

But there ain't no hiding Mr. Hyde

We point the finger

At the fella down the road

"What kind of devil does a thing like that?" we joke

Oh baby, just give it time

Cause we act like Dr. Jekyll

But there ain't no hiding Mr. Hyde

Jesus did not die on the cross to take pretty good people and make them a little bit better. He died to put our sinfulness to death and raise us to new life.

<u>Quest of the Day</u>

1. Play the game Unmatched and choose the character(s) Jekyll & Hyde.

2. Contemplate desires that you are struggling with and deal with them according to Scripture. Confess your sins to God, no matter how small or big. Believe that Jesus is more powerful than your sinful nature. Ask a Christian friend to hold you accountable.

3. Read Romans 6.

DAY 4 — LONDO MOLLARI: KILL THE KEEPER BY NICK HAYDEN

We know that our old self was crucified with [Jesus] in order that the body of sin might be brought to nothing, so that we would no longer be enslaved to sin.

Romans 6:6 (ESV)

The five-season space opera *Babylon 5* is populated by complicated characters, humans and aliens, who change, sometimes in drastic ways, as local and interstellar wars and politics usher in the Third Age of mankind. One of the most intriguing and complicated characters is Londo Mollari. He starts the show as the unserious and often drunk Centauri ambassador. The Centauri are a humanoid race whose empire has fallen from its greatness. Londo's great desire is to restore the glory of the Centauri Republic.

This desire leads him to make dangerous alliances and to be party to genocidal acts. The consequences of these choices follow him even after he repents.

He is saddled with a Keeper by his old allies. A Keeper is a creature that hooks into the neural system of its host and controls it. Londo spends the last years of his life doing the wishes of his Keeper, perpetuating war and suffering on his home planet in the cause of his old allies. He is forced to injure the very people he most wanted to return to glory.

What Paul writes in Romans 7 is true of Londo: "For I do not do the good I want, but the evil I do not want is what I keep on doing. Now if I do what I do not want, it is no longer I who do it, but sin that dwells within me" (19-20).

This is a terrible fate, to do not as you wish but only as the evil attached to you, the evil that has its tendrils wrapped about the most basic parts of you, bids. This is the power of sin in an unbeliever. He is a slave to sin.

Londo's Keeper could not be removed without killing Londo, and we cannot remove the shackles of sin without also dying. That is one of the great truths of the book of Romans-- that we *have* died with Christ, that when Jesus died on the cross, He did not just forgive your sins, but He also severed sin's grasping, clinging, intertwining hold on us.

We still sin, yes, but we do not *have* to sin. The Keeper is dead. We can freely follow Jesus. We can worship God in spirit and in truth. We are free men and women.

Londo Mollari is ultimately a tragic character. His own ambition when free led him to an end where he was kept always under the power of those who hated him, to serve them and to do their will. He did not escape. But by God's mercy we have been freed. Our sin has been crucified, so that no matter our past, no matter our current struggles with sin, we can give ourselves to God and learn to do His will.

Quest of the Day

1. Do you believe you are free from sin's domination? If you have a regular sin you struggle with, remind yourself that the struggle is not hopeless. As Paul says after recounting his own struggles: "Wretched man that I am! Who will deliver me from this body of death? Thanks be to God through Jesus Christ our Lord" (Romans 7:24-25)! Spend time thanking God that "[t]here is therefore now no condemnation for those who are in Christ Jesus" (Romans 8:1). Be specific about those sins that Christ no longer condemns you for.

2. Read Romans 8:1-11.

DAY 5 - BECOMING A DRAGON: THE REDEMPTION OF EUSTACE SCRUBB BY CHRIS COOKE

For he has rescued us from the dominion of darkness and brought us into the kingdom of the Son he loves, in whom we have redemption, the forgiveness of sins.

Colossians 1:13-14

There was a boy named Eustace Clarence Scrubb, and he didn't deserve it. None of us do.

Eustace Scrubb, in both the film and the book versions of *Voyage of the Dawn Treader* was simply the worst. Unlike Edmund in the most famous of the chronicles, *The Lion, The Witch, and The Wardrobe*, he is not shown with any positive or sympathetic qualities. With Edmund, we see him struggling with being separated from his father, who was fighting in the War, and his mother as he and his siblings are sent into the countryside. We see him lashing out at Peter for, as Edmund saw it, "trying to be dad," and being mean to Lucy. But we also see him hurting and feeling out of place in his family. These are things we can see informing his bad actions. Our boy Eustace, though, has none of those aspects. He starts as a tormentor and an overbearing nuisance.

Eustace is well-read, as he spent much of his time studying and reading about "exports and imports and

21

governments and drains." He considers himself learned and in many ways superior to others. This was particularly the case for his cousins, the aforementioned Edmund and Lucy, whom he looks down on for believing in imaginary things and fairy-tales like Narnia. He fancies himself an intellectual; he knows "how the world worked." He looks at things with intense pragmatism and without empathy. When reprimanded for his self-centered attitude, he could convince himself that it was no fault of his own; it is the others treating him awfully. He is innocent, they just can't see it. He knows that they "were really fiends." He believes all of his actions are justified. If there is a water shortage, he could take an extra glass because "a doctor would tell a sick person to drink." He would hide so he could sleep and come back *after* the crew finished setting up camp (thus avoiding helping and working). And of course, he tries to hoard what, unbeknownst to him, is a cursed dragon's treasure. It is here where our boy gets his comeuppance, and much more importantly, where he starts becoming redeemed and sanctified.

You see, upon entering the dragon's lair and trying to hoard as much gold as possible, he puts on a bracelet, which transforms him into a dragon himself. After becoming a dragon, Eustace for the first time realizes his shortcomings and that his cousins, Caspian, and the crew are good people. Becoming a dragon forces Eustace to humble himself. He can't speak, so that first meeting where the crew thinks the dragon killed him is particularly tricky. From there, Eustace eagerly tries in earnest to help the others as much as possible. He shows repentance and becomes a crucial part of the crew— even though he knows he's a challenge as a dragon ("How will we feed him? Do we have room for him?") Eustace is remorseful about how he used to be and wishes he could go back to being a human.

Later on, he meets Aslan at night. Aslan scratches the scales off Eustace and turns him back into a boy. Eustace's growth and Aslan's forgiveness of him is an excellent display of part of the Word:

> The Lord is not slow in keeping his promise, as some understand slowness. Instead he is patient with you, not wanting anyone to perish, but everyone to come to repentance (2 Peter 3:9).

Eustace, like us, was offered a forgiveness and grace that he didn't deserve, and could never earn. He was redeemed by Aslan, as we are redeemed through Christ. Like Eustace, we have been given well beyond a second chance. We've all been rescued from our former sinful selves. We've been forgiven for our transgressions. Like having our scales scratched off, we've been painfully and beautifully sanctified to be made into an image of Christ (which I seriously cannot ever get over). We've been allowed to experience repercussions for our actions, learn from them, and become more like Christ after them.

And further, Eustace wasn't just magically a 1,000% different character and perfect from that point on. Redemption and sanctification for him, was a process, as we read in C.S. Lewis's book:

> It would be nice, and fairly nearly true, to say that "from that time forth Eustace was a different boy." To be strictly accurate, he began to be a different boy. He had relapses. There were still many days when he could be very tiresome. But most of those I shall not notice.
>
> The cure had begun.

Like us, he still struggled and stumbled, but he was changing into a new person, one who was totally unrecognizable to others upon his return from Narnia at the end of the novel and into its sequel, *The Silver Chair*. Now, I know that at the start of this devo I may have seemed harsh on our boy, but there was a reason. The first is I *love* this character, warts and all. The second is that a lot of Eustace's attitudes and traits are ones that I, and many of us, can still struggle with. But then we're wonderfully reminded about the forgiveness and redemption we have in Jesus. This story turns my eyes, mind, and heart to Him, and I'm very thankful for that.

And with that, I'll leave you with the inspiring words

of our favorite Lion: "Courage, dear heart."

For Narnia, and for Aslan!

<u>Quest of the day:</u>

- Take some time to consider the following questions:

    a) What's making me a dragon?

    b) What do I need to repent of?

    c) And how can I help (or how/where can the Lord use me) my community today?

DAY 6 - SAILOR MOON AND A MOON CRISIS OF IDENTITY!
BY BECKY SMITH

Therefore, if anyone is in Christ, the new creation has come:

The old has gone, the new is here!

2 Corinthians 5:17

Sailor Moon, the iconic magical girl. The show that birthed an entire generation of anime fans, and the show that inflamed my budding love for Japanimation (as it was commonly called in the '90s). Even if you've never watched it, you probably know of it and most likely know someone who has watched it.

The story of Sailor Moon centers around a fourteen-year-old girl named Usagi Tsukino (or Serena, or Bunny, depending on the dub or translation). She's the oldest child in her family, a big sister to a younger brother, and the only daughter to her loving and hardworking parents. She's clumsy, lazy, a bit of a dimwit in school, self-indulgent, and overall a brat. Typical teenager, right?

One day, on her way to school, Usagi encounters a group of boys picking on a small black cat. She chases them away and removes the bandage that was stuck to the cat's forehead. The frightened cat jumps away, but not before Usagi sees the moon-shaped mark that was covered by the bandage.

That evening, the same cat appears to Usagi in her bedroom and begins to talk(!). The cat reveals to Usagi that she is none other than Sailor Moon, a Guardian of the Moon Kingdom destined to fight evil. Many adventures and dangers follow, including meeting other Sailor Guardians (some early English translations called them Scouts) and a mysterious cloaked figure named Tuxedo Mask, who always appears just when things get too tough for Sailor Moon.

Throughout the series, we get to witness Usagi grow into her new identity and struggle as she discovers that she's not only a Sailor Guardian, but she's also the Princess of the Moon Kingdom named Princess Serenity (how many names can one girl have?) and the mother of the time-traveling Chibiusa. Each new revelation of her true identity leaves Usagi reeling in confusion as she comes to grips with all the different aspects of being a Guardian, a princess, and a mother. She's just a teenage girl after all. She'd rather be eating cake and reading manga!

This leads to our topic in today's devotional: identity. Identity is a big controversial issue in this day and age. Who am I? What am I? How does this impact my everyday life? How can I be happy with myself? These big questions can leave a person, not unlike Usagi, reeling in doubt, confusion, and in extreme cases, despair. In this world of shifting ideas about identity, it can become a heavy burden to constantly be questioning, let alone seeking affirmation of, your identity. Depression, an overall sense of discontentment, and the feeling of being lost can hold sway over our hearts and minds. As Christians, how do we combat this?

We'll be doing a bit of reading, so let's pull out our transformation pens...I mean, the Scriptures, and see what God has to say!

Psalm 33:6-9: The Psalms are a great place to start. They cover just about every topic we could possibly need as we learn more about God. Psalm 33 is a song of praise to the Lord, and in these three verses, it tells us that we should praise God for His Creation. He created all we see (the Earth and the heavens) and holds it all together.

- **Psalm 139:13-16:** This song written by David gets a little more personal. David rightfully attributes God with his very existence. He uses the words "fearfully and wonderfully" because at the same time he recognizes the frailty of being human as well as the joys of living.

- **Colossians 1:16-17:** Moving into the New Testament, we have a passage that is explicit regarding the nature of Jesus's divinity and how it is through him that all things were created and that they were created for Him. In case you haven't noticed, I'm building my case for why we should be looking to God to find out who we are. If He is our creator and sustainer, and we were made for Him, then it only follows that it is He who gives us our identity. What identity is that? Let's take a look at a couple more passages.

- **Romans 6:6-11 and Ephesians 2:1-6:** Paul is the author of both of these passages and makes a very clear case for what should be our new identity, or *who*, rather. It's Jesus! As born again children of God, we are in Christ and we get to share in all that that entails! New life, a new home, new family, new blessings and all for eternity! There is no better identity than to have the one that is given to us by our Heavenly Father through Christ.

The Bible is the story of countless individuals who suffer from having the wrong identity or no identity at all and being given a new and better identity through the work and person of Jesus Christ. We are part of that story. Christian, be encouraged today knowing that when you question who you are, you can turn to the Scriptures and to God for the answer. Your new and better identity, your heavenly identity, is in Christ, and it will never change.

Quests of the Day

1. Write down all the blessings you receive in Christ.

2. Write down all the different aspects of your earthly identity that trouble you.

3. Pray over both lists, thanking God for the blessings He's given you in Christ and asking Him for guidance and peace over your temporal, earthly identity.

<u>Bonus Side Quest</u>

If you would like to see an early version of this devotional, I did a video for my friends Dallas and Celeste over at Geek Devotions on YouTube back in 2018. It is called "Where Does Your Real Identity Come From?" So, head on over to YouTube and check it out!

DAY 7 - BE INCREDIBLE! (THE INCREDIBLES) BY SCOTT BAYLES

God has given each of you a gift from his great variety of
spiritual gifts. Use them well to serve one another.

1 Peter 4:10 NLT

Everyone loves superheroes. Except, that is, the good
people of Metroville, the fictional setting of Pixar's beloved
box-office smash, *The Incredibles*. The city of Metroville has
been slapped with so many lawsuits from property owners,
people injured during rescues and suicidal citizens who didn't
want to be saved, that it has forced caped crusaders and
superpowered defenders of justice into early retirement. After
fifteen years of said forced retirement, Bob and Helen—once
known to the world as Mr. Incredible and Elastigirl—struggle
to live "normal" lives in the suburbs along with their three kids,
Violet, Dash, and baby Jack-Jack.

Each member of this incredible family possesses
unique powers and abilities. Mr. Incredible, or Bob, employs
unmatched super-strength. Elastigirl, or Helen, can stretch and
twist her body into infinite shapes. Their daughter, Violet, can
turn invisible and generate forcefields. Dash, like his name
suggests, sprints at unbelievable speeds. Even baby Jack-Jack
possesses bizarre transformative powers. And let's not forget

Bob's buddy, Frozone, who can shoot ice from his hands and ride on waves of self-made snow.

Their powers and abilities make them unique…special. However, living in a world where they must hide their powers takes a toll on the family. Bob feels discouraged and depressed, packing on the pounds in a corporate cubicle, living the subdued life of an insurance claims adjuster. At home, he's disinterested and detached at the dinner table. The whole family experiences similar problems. Violet feels invisible and tried to fade into the background. Dash gets in trouble at school for pulling super-speed stunts, because he doesn't have a healthy outlet for his powers. Helen and Bob both appear dissatisfied and discouraged with their average, ordinary lives.

When Helen reminds Dash about the importance of keeping his powers a secret, he whines, "But Dad always said our powers were nothing to be ashamed of, our powers made us special." To which Helen replies, "Everyone's special, Dash." Then Dash mutters, "Which is another way of saying no one is."

The villain of the story expresses the same twisted perspective. After using technology that he invented to give himself the equivalent of superpowers, Syndrome brags to a defeated Mr. Incredible, "I did it without your precious gifts, your oh-so-special powers…. And when I'm old and I've had my fun, I'll sell my inventions so that everyone can be superheroes. Everyone can be super! And when everyone's super...no one will be."

Syndrome and Dash made the same mistake. They didn't realize that both Helen and Bob were right. Their unique powers and abilities *do* make them special. But since no one has precisely the same superpowers, everyone is special their own unique way.

The same is true for you and me. Although we don't possess superpowers, God has given each one of us special abilities called spiritual gifts. Here's what the Bible says:

> In his grace, God has given us different gifts for doing certain things well. So if God has given you the ability to prophesy, speak out with as much faith as God has given you. If your gift is serving others, serve them well. If you are a teacher, teach well. If your gift is to encourage others, be encouraging. If it is giving, give generously. If God has given you leadership ability, take the responsibility seriously. And if you have a gift for showing kindness to others, do it gladly (Romans 12:6-8 NLT).

This list is far from exhaustive, by the way. Four similar passages identify other spiritual gifts, too. But this represents a sample of the kind of spiritual gifts God gives. Because the

Holy Spirit loves variety and wants us to be special, no single gift is given to everyone and no single person received all the gifts; rather every gift or set of gifts is unique. That's what makes us special. Our job is to discover and develop our gifts. Identifying and utilizing your spiritual gifts is one of the most exciting spiritual adventures a person can experience.

When the Incredible family begins using their powers to fight evil and save people, things begin to change. Bob immediately starts getting in shape. There's a spring in his step and smile on his face. He dances with Helen in the living room. Violet stops hiding her face behind her hair and finds the courage to talk to a boy she likes. Dash tries out for the track team. By embracing their gifts and using them to help others, the Incredibles experience renewed contentment and confidence.

I think the same thing happens to Christians when they start using their gifts to help others. The Holy Spirit doesn't just give us these gifts for our own enjoyment; rather He gives to us so that we can give to others. Paul writes, "A spiritual gift is given to each of us so we can help each other" (1 Corinthians 12:7 NLT). Peter puts it this way: "God has given each of you a gift from his great variety of spiritual gifts. Use them well to serve one another" (1 Peter 4:10 NLT).

The Holy Spirit intends for us to use the gifts He has given us for the common good, to help one another, and build up the entire church. Doing so gives us a sense of purpose and leads to a life of fulfillment. If we will commit to discovering and developing the spiritual gifts God gives us and use them to selflessly serve others, then we just might become *incredible* followers of Christ!

Quest of the Day

1. Read Romans 12:6–8, 1 Corinthians 12:8–10, and 1 Peter 4:11.

2. If you could have any superpower what would it be and how would you use it?

3. What spiritual gifts has God given you? How can you use your gifts to serve your church and/or community?

4. If you're not already volunteering in your church, talk to your pastor or other church leader about ways you can use your gifts to serve.

DAY 8 – ATRUS AND THE ART OF MANKIND BY NICK HAYDEN

In the beginning, God created the heavens and the earth.

Genesis 1:1

Myst is my kind of game. You play a nameless protagonist who discovers a book that links you to an island. Here, there are more Linking Books, each leading to an Age, a small self-contained world that you must explore to find the Linking Book back to the original island, Myst. Each Age is filled with puzzles that are naturally embedded in each Age. Released in 1993, it was the bestselling computer game until 2002, when it was surpassed by *The Sims*.

Myst satisfies my itch for both challenging puzzles and interesting worlds to explore, but through the sequels and several books, those interested in the world of Myst are introduced to Atrus, who created the Linking Books, and to the D'ni, the people who created the Art of writing worlds into existence. Atrus's sons use the Art to make ages where they can play out their greed and brutality, and Atrus's father saw the Art as a way to have God-like powers, but Atrus himself treats the Art with respect, believing that the worlds he writes are not created by him but are only descriptions of worlds already created by the Maker. His Art is to write into being worlds that already existed. He is, in some sense, a fellow creator with the Maker Himself.

And so are we.

The first thing we learn about God in the Bible is that he is a Creator. He makes the heavens and the earth; He makes light and water and land and plant and beast and human. God is much more than a Creator, of course, but He is not less than one. Jesus was a carpenter, after all.

So when we read in Genesis 1:27 that "God created man in his own image, in the image of God he created him; male and female he created them," that image includes, at the very least, the desire and ability and privilege to create. He made us to come alongside Him and participate in forming the world He gave us.

Creating might mean writing (as I'm doing at this very moment). It might mean some other fine art like drawing or singing. But it might mean tinkering with engines or weeding a garden or organizing a sock drawer. It means nurturing friendships and starting book clubs and raising kids. It means putting a vase of flowers on a table to beautify a room, and it means picking up litter from the sidewalk.

Atrus has the mystical ability to put special ink to special paper, and by writing special words in this ink on this paper, he can usher a pocket world into existence. And that's super cool. But coders do the same things with bytes, and cooks with herbs and spices, and preschool teachers with the chaos that is a three-year-old. We all have the ability to bring order from chaos.

Before we were told to "go, and make disciples of all nations," we were told to "be fruitful and multiply and fill the earth and subdue it." We were told to create something beautiful and orderly and true from what God has graciously given us. So, go mend a shirt or start a soup kitchen or learn to whittle. (And also, make disciples.) You were made to create, to tend the garden of where you live. This glorifies God.

It's rather exciting, isn't it?

Quest of the Day

1. What is one way you naturally create? It doesn't have to be big or important. If you write music, awesome. If you write letters to friends on their birthday, awesome. Thank God for this creative outlet. When you do it next, be aware it is from him and can be used to glorify him.

2. What's one area in your normal sphere of influence where you could create in a new way? Again, this doesn't have to be big. Maybe it's painting a rundown deck or reconnecting with old friends. Do it.

3. If your creation is one that can be shared, do so over social media, with the hashtag #42terraforming.

DAY 9 – TONANE AND AWARENESS
BY ERIC ANDERSON

Let us then approach God's throne of grace with confidence, so that we may receive mercy and find grace to help us in our time of need.

Hebrews 4:16

Have you ever met Tonane? Oh, you would like him. Tonane is a calm, friendly man who is part of a Native American tribe called the Salish. In the *Stargate SG-1* episode "Spirits" (Season 2, Ep. 13), the team, minus Jack O'Neill, meets him when they travel through a device called a stargate to a planet designated PXY-887. They go to the planet unaware that it is inhabited because SG-11 has disappeared. After being shot with poison darts, the team wakes up in a building built with "trinium," a mineral on the planet that SG-11 was looking into mining as a resource. Tonane comes to meet them. The tribe had been there for many years after the Goa'uld (the bad guys) had brought them there. Then some "spirits" had rescued them and protected them for at least a thousand years.

Tonane explains to SG-1 that they are not prisoners and immediately gives them their weapons back. When they ask about SG-11, he says he does not know where they are. He says, "The Spirits know. We can go and ask them." As they walk out of the camp, Daniel starts explaining to Sam that they might be asked to do a ceremonial dance, but then Tonane starts calling out "X'els," the name of the lead spirit.

Daniel: Uh, wait, aren't you going to do a ceremonial dance or...something?

Tonane: My great, great grandfather used to call the spirits that way, but one day X'els just said, "Call my name." That's what we do.

(Soon a wolf comes out into the path).

Tonane: T'akaya, my friend! My! Your coat shines beautifully today. A little flattery couldn't hurt, Sam.

Carter: My! What big eyes you have!

Tonane: Ask her about your friends.

Carter: T'akaya...do you think our friends might be [sighs]....

Tonane: She's right there.

Carter: I can only see a wolf, Tonane. A beautiful animal, granted, but not a spirit.

Tonane: You can't see the wind, either, Sam. But you know it's there. You can hear it. You can feel it. You can see its effects on the trees. It's the same with the spirits. You see a wolf, but T'akaya is there.

When a raven flies to a nearby branch, Daniel asks Tonane if it is X'els, the lead spirit. He says, "Yes," and Daniel, with a small sense of confidence, requests that their friends be returned to them. The raven then caws, and Daniel, with support from Teal'c, claims it is saying, "Yes," while Tonane thinks X'els is saying he will think about it. Throughout the episode, Tonane shows a firm trust in these spirits.

What I love about Tonane is his firm confidence that he can simply walk into the woods and call for X'els and/or T'akaya. We get no sense that the idea of being ignored is even a thought in his mind. He does not see these spirits as aloof and uninvolved but as available. He sees them as friends or protectors who want to meet with him.

Major Carter, with a keen scientific mind, could not imagine that a spirit would just be there. In her mind, if you see a wolf, you have a wolf. She has no confidence that the spirits are there, no thought that they would appear as animals. Having met Goa'ulds who pose as deities, she was expecting either nothing or a humanoid person with technology.

Genesis 2 records that God, after forming Adam, brought him many animals and watched to see what he would call them. We get a sense that God had a relationship with Adam; that He would come and meet with him in the garden. Then in Genesis 3:8, we read that Adam and Eve "heard the sound of the Lord God as he was walking in the garden in the cool of the day...." This is when they hid from him. They had met another being that day: a serpent that successfully tempted them into eating fruit from the one tree they were told not to eat from.

We tend to see God as far separated from us, like a far-off being who is just there to judge us. But what Adam and Eve found was a God of forgiveness. You see, God found them, let them explain what was going on, and then made clothes for them. God wanted to talk to them. He wanted to hear their side of the story. He did correct them. He certainly disapproved of the disobedience, and even kicked the couple out of the Garden He had made for them. By making them clothes from garments of skin, He had acted as their priest, making the first sacrifice to pay for redemption.

Take notice that they heard Him walking and hid. Not in the sense of "who is that?", but in the sense of, "oh, *He* is coming." They recognized the presence of God, and it is strongly insinuated that this was common for them. Just as Tonane was so accustomed to the spirits that he recognized them easily, so did Adam and Eve recognize their Creator when He came to them.

Prayer does not need to be a huge production, and I write that as a guy who loves doing lighting for worship with colors that fit the songs and movement during the exciting moments. There is a place for large worship production (see 1 Chronicles 15:16, Psalm 149, and Psalm 150). Prayer is about walking "into the woods" and calling for Christ. Hebrews 4:16 tells us to "...approach God's throne of Grace with confidence, so that we may receive mercy and find grace...."

In Tonane's interactions with T'akaya and X'els, we see that he recognizes who they are. He compliments T'akaya on her coat of fur and tells Sam to use flattery. Spoiler: the spirits are shapeshifting aliens. Eventually Tonane goes with SG-1 back to the SGC, and toward the end of the episode when Tonane finds out they are shapeshifters, he is asked what form his people prefer. "You have always been kind to my people, so whatever makes you happy." He knows that these creatures have protected him and his people.

God is not a shapeshifting alien, but He does enjoy talking with us. He is available at all times, even at "o dark thirty." He is available in all places: in the shower, on the road (but don't be distracted while driving), and at the movie theater. Even if we colonize other planets with ships or through stargates, He will still find us. We are safe with our God in the gardens, in a war, and in everything in between.

Quest of the Day

1. Read Psalm 139.
2. Take a walk and have a conversation with God.
    a. Just call His name (Jesus, Yahweh, Father God)
    b. Compliment Him (aka worship).
    c. Ask Him to help your friends.
    d. Ask Him to help people you don't know.
    e. Ask Him to help you.

DAY 10 - FROM BRIGHTEST DAY TO BLACKEST NIGHT: JESSICA CRUZ, THE ANXIETY LANTERN BY CHRIS COOKE

Peace I leave with you; my peace I give you. I do not give to you as the world gives. Do not let your hearts be troubled and do not be afraid.

John 14:27

Comics are a funny thing. They're one of my favorite mediums. Most of the time, the stories they tell are of the extreme fantastical variety, where the world (or galaxy or universe or multiverse) hangs in the balance (like DC's various *Crisis* titles and Marvel's *Infinity* stories), where no one except Uncle Ben Parker stays dead, where clones exist in overblown sagas (like Marvel's *Second Clone Saga*), and where you can kill a Robin and then Batman can't touch you because you're suddenly the ambassador to Iran and have diplomatic immunity (*A Death In The Family*). But sometimes you get more grounded and personal stories: Matt Murdock's crisis of faith (*Born Again*), Tony Stark's struggles with sobriety (*Demon in the Bottle*), Batman's intense obsession and need to honor his parents (er...basically any Batman story). And then are times where you get stories and characters so good, they punch you in the face. That character is Jessica Cruz, and that story is *Green Lanterns*, Volume One, #15.

But before I get into this fantastic issue, let's briefly talk about Jess, because unless you follow the comics or the straight-to-DVD DC animated movies, you might only know Hal Jordan as the Green Lantern. Jess was fully introduced back in 2014 in *Justice League*, Volume Two, #31. What makes Jess stand out, aside from being the first human woman Green Lantern and her multicultural heritage, is her struggle with anxiety disorder. Anxiety is something many of us struggle with, but not until the last 10 years has it been so openly talked about, and as someone who struggles with general anxiety, seeing a superhero struggle with it in an ongoing capacity has been wonderful. With Jess, though, this struggle is on a different level. If you're not aware, in the early 2000's, Geoff Johns added meanings behind the Lanterns' colors and powers. Before then, it used to be that the Green Lanterns were weak against the color yellow for no real reason. But then Mr. Johns added meaning: green represented willpower, and only those with the strongest wills could use it. Yellow represented fear, which could undo willpower. This ties into Jess perfectly, as she struggles with being a Green Lantern. At times she's fine; she can take on a foe that attacks Superman head-on. But then at other times, she has difficulty with street-level henchmen.

Her struggles and victories with her anxiety is a constant part of her story, and it is perhaps best displayed in her team-up series with fellow Lantern Simon Boaz in *Green Lanterns*, Volume one, #15. In this issue, we get an amazing glimpse into what struggling with anxiety looks like. How it's not just a one-and-done incident. How sometimes right after we face it and win against something huge, something small can set us off and send us spiraling. How the biggest battle can be to get out of bed, let alone out of our heads. For someone with anxiety, this issue depicts the daily struggles, feelings, and spiraling (when it happens) perfectly. And just when I thought it couldn't get any better, Jessica says,

> Stop. Do your breathing. Ground yourself.
> These are just thoughts. I am not my thoughts.
> I am not my worst fears. I defy fear. I'm a
> Green Lantern. Bit by bit. Step by step. Chip
> away at the fear. You can do this.

Our girl Jess pulls it together "bit by bit, step by step." This quotation and the accompanying panels are a borderline instruction manual for when anxiety hits.

However, there are some things I've added for myself that help me, and hopefully they'll encourage you too.

- **"Stop. Do your breathing"** and *pray.* Praying gets *you out of your head,* and s*ets your mind towards God,* who is much better to have your mind on and is the best audience to cast your anxieties onto.

- **"Ground yourself"** *in the Word.* Knowing what the Scriptures say can be a huge asset when spiraling. It will be an anchor for you and turn your eyes and mind to Him. Some that I've memorized and used in this practice are 1 Peter 5:7, Philippians 4:13, and Hebrews 13:6.

- **"These are just thoughts. I am not my thoughts. I am not my worst fears,"** I am *fearfully and wonderfully made (Psalm 139:14).* **"I defy fear."** *I'm a child of God, and I can be a force of good for His glory.*

Be like our girl, Jess. Get out of bed, grab your Power Ring (or the more powerful Bible), face your fears...and get some breakfast. It's what she does at the end of the issue. And you can never go wrong with breakfast food.

Quest of the Day

1. Seek out Scriptures that provide you comfort and start committing them to memory or add them to a place you have easy access too for times of stress.

2. Learn what helps you during times of attack—rocking out to a song, playing ping-pong, calling on a friend, whatever it is—and ask the Lord to always present a way away from the situation when needed.

3. Put these into practice, and after a week see if things have improved.

DAY 11 – FANTASTIC FOUR: A FANTASTIC FAMILY!
BY SCOTT BAYLES

God decided in advance to adopt us into his own family by
bringing us to himself through Jesus Christ.

Ephesians 1:5 NLT

In 1961, the legendary Stan Lee created Marvel's First
Family. Their story began with the inaugural test flight of a
space shuttle designed by Reed Richards, one of the world's
foremost scientific minds. During the mission, cosmic rays
bombard the ship and force it to crash land back on Earth,
where Reed, his then-girlfriend Sue Storm, her brother Johnny
Storm, and test pilot Ben Grimm emerge from the wreckage
to discover they had been miraculously endowed with fantastic
abilities. Reed becomes the super-stretchy Mr. Fantastic. Ben
transforms into the "ever-lovin' blue-eyed" Thing. Sue turns
transparent and chooses the codename Invisible Girl. And
Johnny bursts into flames as the Human Torch. Together they
form the Fantastic Four.

For more than fifty-five years, the Fantastic Four
enjoyed uninterrupted publication and popularity. But when
Marvel Studios entered a heated battle with 20th Century Fox
over the movie rights to these beloved characters, the
adventures of the Fantastic Four came to an end. The team

fractured when Reed and Sue, who had since married, along with their son and daughter, disappeared—presumed dead by their teammates, and Marvel cancelled their ongoing comic series.

After a three-year hiatus, though, Marvel finally regained the movie rights to their characters and relaunched the *Fantastic Four* comic books.

The opening story arc of this new series reminds readers that the Fantastic Four is more than a team—it's a family. In the introductory narration, Sue Richards says, "Who are we? It's simple…Me. The man I love. My brother. Our best friend. We are adventurers. And we're on the greatest adventure of all. Being part of a family."

It turns out that Reed and Sue, as well as their children, are alive and well, and experiencing grand adventures across the multiverse until they encounter a celestial being who calls herself the Griever—the living embodiment of destruction. Griever's sole purpose is to unravel the fabric of every universe, resulting in total entropy.

After thoroughly thrashing the Richardses, Griever gloats, "To think that this was the great Fantastic Four. The legendary heroes spoken about across all corners of creation. I expected so much more."

Reed responds defiantly, "No, Griever. If the rest of my family were here…if you had faced all of the Fantastic Four, we would have defeated you. Easily."

Insulted by Reed's impudence, Griever commands, "Go. Summon your Fantastic Four and I shall lay them low as well."

Griever then allows Reed to build a device that will enable him to teleport the rest of the Fantastic Four across the cosmos to face Griever in battle. Sue worries that even their combined might won't be enough to stop Griever, but Reed reminds her, "Have faith…we are so much more than the sum of our parts."

Upon completing the teleportation device, Reed flips a switch, and suddenly the Thing and the Human Torch materialize before them, accompanied by more than a dozen of Earth's superheroes.

"What is this? Deception!" Griever cries.

Reed replies, "No, Griever. This is the Fantastic Four. Meet my family. Or should I say…my extended family!"

Mr. Fantastic cleverly teleported every superhero who ever substituted or temporarily filled the ranks of the Fantastic Four, including Spider-Man, Wolverine, She-Hulk, and many more. Sue announces to the newcomers, "Our multiverse has never faced a greater threat! This is going to take *all* of the Fantastic Four!" While the rest of the team keeps her occupied,

Reed devises a way to send Griever back to her native realm and trap her there for good. Together, the Fantastic Four defeated their foe and saved the multiverse…and they did it as a family.

If you're a believer, then you, like the Fantastic Four, are on the greatest adventure of all: being part of a family—God's family. The Bible uses a whole host of metaphors for the church, but one of the most pervasive is that of family. The church is your extended family. In the New Testament, believers call one another "brother" and "sister." The Bible describes our "adoption" as children of God (Romans 8:14-15). The church is called the "household" of God. The Bible says, "Now you…are not foreigners or strangers any longer, but are citizens together with God's holy people. You belong to God's family" (Ephesians 2:19 NCV).

One of the blessings of belonging to God's family is that we have strength in numbers. None of us can do alone what all of us can do together. Solomon, in his vast wisdom, put it this way: "Two people are better off than one, for they can help each other succeed. If one person falls, the other can reach out and help. But someone who falls alone is in real trouble…. A person standing alone can be attacked and defeated, but two can stand back-to-back and conquer. Three are even better, for a triple-braided cord is not easily broken"

(Ecclesiastes 4:9-12 NLT). Like Reed Richards said, "We are so much more than the sum of our parts."

When you belong to a local body of believers, you have a spiritual family that will support you through difficult times, help you overcome adversity, and work beside you to defeat Satan and save the world by spreading the Gospel. After defeating Griever, the Thing wraps his big, orange arms around Reed and Sue, and says, "Can we go home now? 'Cause I need my family." So do we, big guy. So do we.

Quest of the Day

1. Read Luke 8:19-28.

2. What are some ways the church is like a family? What are some the benefits of belonging to God's family?

3. A believer without a church family is like an orphan. If you don't belong to a local church family, find a church to attend this Sunday. If you do belong to a local church, praise God for your extended family.

DAY 12 – THE UNMATCHED BRUCE LEE: BE WATER, MY FRIEND
BY NATHAN MARCHAND

> I have become all things to all people so that by all possible
> means I might save some.
>
> 1 Cor. 9:22b

If you only know Bruce Lee from his handful of martial arts movies, you'd think he was superhuman. Heck, he was part of the inspiration for the Marvel superhero Iron Fist in 1974. Considering Bruce had the physique of a Greek statue and the ability to play table tennis with nunchakus (and win!), he could've easily cosplayed "the Living Weapon" had he not died tragically the year before.

Bruce wasn't just an actor and martial artist, though. He studied philosophy, among other things, at university. In a 1971 interview with Pierre Berton, Bruce famously restated lines he said in the short-lived TV series *Longstreet* that sum up key facets of his personal philosophy and that of his fighting style, Jeet Kune Do. He said,

> Empty your mind. Be formless, shapeless, like
> water. Now, you put water into a cup, it
> becomes the cup. You put water into a bottle,
> it becomes the bottle. You put it into a teapot,

it becomes the teapot. Now, water can flow or

it can crash. Be water, my friend.

In the original show, he preceded this speech with this line: "Don't get set into one form. Adapt it and build your own, and let it grow. Be like water."

What Bruce was saying was adaptability was necessary in combat. Being set in one particular method or style would hinder performance, and in many cases, make one lose the fight and possibly one's life. Adaptability sped up one's reaction time (and boy, could he punch fast!) and made one a more versatile combatant.

The Apostle Paul did something similar in his ministry. He wrote,

Though I am free and belong to no one, I have made myself a slave to everyone, to win as many as possible. To the Jews I became like a Jew, to win the Jews. To those under the law I became like one under the law (though I myself am not under the law), so as to win those under the law. To those not having the law I became like one not having the law (though I am not free from God's law but am under Christ's law), so as to win those not having the law. To the weak I became weak, to win the weak. I have become all things to

54

all people so that by all possible means I
might save some. I do all this for the sake of
the gospel, that I may share in its blessings (1
Cor. 9:19-23).

Paul didn't impose his freedom in Christ on anyone. He
adjusted his manner depending on who he was interacting
with, so long as it didn't violate Jesus's teachings. If it was Jews
under the Old Testament law, he conducted himself as
someone under that law. If they weren't under the law (i.e.
Gentiles), he didn't act like he was under the law. If he was
around someone with a weak conscience, as he discussed a few
chapters earlier (ch. 8:9-13), he would accommodate them so
as not to be a stumbling block. If they went against their
personal convictions about one thing—such as not eating meat
sacrificed to idols—it would be easier for them to compromise
on the important tenets of their faith. So, Paul gave up some
of his freedom—in other words, he adapted—when the
situation called for it.

The same will and should be true in your interactions
with others. You can't expect non-Christians to live by your
beliefs, so you give them grace. Someone coming from a life
of alcoholism or a family of alcoholics may abstain from "adult
beverages" even though the Bible condemns drunkenness and
not the drinks themselves. Imposing your personal convictions
on these people is a one-way ticket to driving them from the

faith or stunting their spiritual growth. God's work in their lives is far more important than you exercising all of your freedoms all of the time. It's a small price to pay for their wellbeing.

Be water, my friends.

Quest of the Day

1. What are some freedoms you enjoy in Christ? Journal about them.

2. Next, journal about some personal convictions your friends have that don't go against biblical teaching. This could concern things like communion, dress codes, and/or alcohol.

3. Finally, journal about how you can accommodate those people and their consciences when you interact with them. Then go do so.

DAY 13 - DARKWING DUCK SAYS, "I AM..." BY DARRIN BALL

God said to Moses, "I AM WHO I AM… say to the Israelites: 'I AM has sent me to you.' "

Exodus 3:14

"I am the terror that flaps in the night. I am the hairball that clogs in your drain. I am the parking meter that expires while you're shopping. I am Darkwing Duck! Let's get dangerous."

Researching for these devotionals can be painstaking. I'm sitting here in my Darkwing Duck shirt watching episode after episode. This silent scourge stalking his adversaries swoops out of the shadows to rampage rampant rascally robbers. This nocturnal nemesis of ne'er-do-wells precociously pounces upon his putative prey.

Whoa, his narration is rubbing off on me.

This daring dynamic do-gooder with his trusty sidekick, Launchpad McQuack, who is bound at some point each episode to cataclysmically crash, skillfully saves the day from cleverly concocted crime waves, even if it's not quite in the way you (or he) expects. And he takes time to pose for a phenomenal photo-op. *And* this audacious avenger narrates his own action-packed adventures while trashing terrible terrifying terrorists, many times using alliteration. After all, no one else does it justice. "Suck gas, evildoer! Night is my favorite time of day!"

At some point in the episode, DW calls out two or three "I am" lines and then his trademark phrase; something like, "I am the terror that flaps in the night. I am the jailer who throws away the key. I am the termite that devours your floorboards. I am Darkwing Duck. Let's get dangerous."

The thing about his "I am" statements is that they were always relatable; annoying, but relatable. Darkwing would speak in a language that his adversaries could easily understand. We've all had that chill run up our spine. Everyone knows what it's like to have an icky bug crawl up our trouser leg (ah, get it off me!). When the moth circles the flame, we all have that feeling of unease that it will fly right into us, totally creeping us out. Here are a few more of my favorites from DW:

- "I am the flea you cannot flick."
- "I am the ingrown toenail on the foot of crime."
- "I am the repairman who tells you your warranty has run out."

Jesus spoke in a language that people could easily understand. He had several "I AM" statements that describe who He is. Take some time to meditate on the words of Jesus.

- "I AM the bread of life" (John 6:35, 48, 51). Jesus made this statement after He fed five thousand men plus women and children with five loaves of barley

58

bread and two small fish. Before the miracle, they were hungry; afterward they were completely satisfied and couldn't eat another bite. Jesus said that the reason they sought Him out was because they ate and were satisfied. Jesus satisfies. Anything we might be hungry for, Jesus is true satisfaction. Jesus is the bread of life. He brings true meaning and fulfillment to life.

- "I AM the light of the world" (John 8:12, 9:5). Light is something we benefit from every day, unless you are blind. Light shows us the way. Light exposes things, like dirty spots and stains. As the true light of the world, Jesus exposes our sinfulness. If we deny our sinfulness, we remain spiritually blind. Jesus had this very conversation with religious people who thought they were good in John 9:39-41. Without Jesus, we cannot see the way.

- "I AM the gate for the sheep" (John 10:7, 9). This was said when shepherds and sheep were an everyday sight. There was only one entrance where sheep would enter into a pen. The shepherd himself would stand there, allowing entrance to his sheep only. The only way to enter into belonging to God is through Jesus Christ. He stands there allowing entrance only to those who belong to Him.

- "I AM the good shepherd" (John 10:11, 14). A good shepherd risks his life for his sheep. Others only come to steal, kill, and destroy. Jesus, on the other hand, comes that we might have a full, abundant life. Jesus only wants your good. As the good shepherd, He lays down His life for you. The enemy will always take from you. Jesus only gives, and He gave His own life first.

- "I AM the resurrection and the life" (John 11:25). In this story, Jesus was about to bring back to life Lazarus, a close friend of His, who had been dead and in the tomb for four days. He announced that He is the resurrection and the life and asks if Martha believes this. (Before Jesus does anything for you, do you believe that He is who He says He is?) Then, to prove beyond all doubt, He calls to Lazarus, "Come forth!" Lazarus walked out of the tomb. The resurrection is not just an event. The resurrection is a person, Jesus Christ. We haven't witnessed these miracles, but like Martha, we are called to believe before we see anything miraculous.

- "I AM the way and the truth and the life" (John 14:6). The ironic fact about this statement is that it was given to His disciples who had known Jesus for quite some time. Yet they still grappled with His true identity. Thomas asked, "Lord, we don't know where you are going, so how can we know the way?" This simple statement of Jesus is so profound, we could ponder it for days. "I AM the way." It's not a question of knowing a path through life. It's about knowing a person, Jesus Christ. If we know Him, we have the truth and eternal life. All the fullness of God is in the person of Jesus (Colossians 2:9).

- "I AM the true vine" (John 15:1, 5). It's possible that Jesus and His disciples were walking through a vineyard as He spoke this, since He had just commanded them to get up and go somewhere else (John 14:31). Jesus said, "I AM the vine; you are the branches." There is no life for the branches outside of the vine. No branch can bear fruit if it does not abide in the vine. In the same way, we have no life outside of Jesus Christ. Nothing of any value will grow in our lives if we do not abide in Him.

- "Before Abraham was born, I AM" (John 8:58). Maybe all of them aren't easy to understand. Perhaps there is a mystery to this man who is also God. Abraham lived a couple thousand years before Jesus, and yet Jesus stated that He pre-existed Abraham. Even in His pre-incarnate state Jesus spoke of Himself in the present tense. In Revelation 1:8 and 22:13, the glorified Jesus Christ revealed, "I AM...the beginning, I AM...the ending." He didn't say that He *was* the beginning and He *will be* the ending. It's always present tense. I AM. *For the believer, Jesus is always present reality.*

How about Darkwing Duck's phrase, "Let's get dangerous"? Is there a spiritual application? Ummm…maybe for the next 42 devotional.

<u>Quest of the Day</u>

1. Buy a Darkwing Duck DVD on eBay and watch an episode or watch the show on Disney+.

2. Read John 11. What comes first in your life, belief or proof? Journal about times when you have exercised faith. That is, believing without seeing.

3. Talk with a close friend about one or more of these I AM statements and how your understanding of Christ is more complete because of that statement.

DAY 14 – MERLIN THE FOOL
BY ERIC ANDERSON

For the message of the cross is foolishness to those who are perishing, but to us who are being saved it is the power of God.

1 Corinthians 1:18

Merlin is an extraordinary mythical figure. In the legends, he is an old man who acts as a magician and mentor to King Arthur (as well as his father, Uther Pendragon) and uses his spells to support the kingdom in many ways. For the purposes of today's entry, we will look at the version based on my second favorite BBC show. In the adventure series *Merlin*, we find a young magician caught living in the Kingdom of Camelot played by Colin Morgan. Not only is Merlin young, but magic is quite illegal, having been outlawed by Uther Pendragon because of attacks by those who use magic not for good but for ill. Merlin comes to Camelot seeking a mentor. Specifically, he comes to Gaius, the King's physician.

We find Merlin inexperienced, rash, and foolish, yet in the first episode he saves the lives of many when a young girl seeks revenge on the court. She uses magical abilities to put everyone to sleep, and Merlin is the one person who realizes what is actually happening. As his "prize" for saving lives, he is given the role of Arthur's manservant. So, he is adjacent to the court, having to keep secret his amazing abilities, which he does not yet understand, while serving a man who at this point has no respect for him. This is an odd take on the story, but it teaches much over the course of the series.

As the story moves on, Merlin learns and grows into a mighty magician but still must often play the fool. He often is late for this or that and is quite frustrating for Arthur and even Gaius just because he has much on his plate and must hide his abilities. Eventually, he becomes a fool more akin to what you find in Shakespeare's plays. In such stories, the Fool of the court is often the smartest person in the room. In this case, Merlin has a mission he is on to protect Arthur and Camelot even when the Knights see him as the boy who cleans the dishes on their journeys. The Apostle Paul once spoke of such things:

> Brothers and sisters, think of what you were when you called. Not many of you were wise by human standards; not many were influential; not many were of noble birth. But God chose the foolish things of the world to shame the wise; God chose the weak things of the world to shame the strong" (1 Corinthians 1:26-27).

While wisdom is counted as a gift from God, sometimes He chooses to shine by using someone or something foolish. He can take that which is foolish and change hearts and that which is weak and change planets. Do you ever feel like others look down on you as "foolish" because of your faith in Christ? Jesus himself experienced this. None of his disciples understood the multiple times when He told them about his coming death. It was confusing to them as to why Jesus would be killed when he had the power to heal the sick or even raise the dead. When facing trial, He was quiet and did nothing to defend Himself. He knew the the plan God the Father laid out included this humiliating death, and He "...endured the cross, scorning its shame and sat down at the right hand of the throne of God" (Hebrews 12:2). Jesus willingly allowed Himself to look a fool in order to complete the most important mission of all time: redeeming us from all our sin. Then he proved the confused and the arrogant wrong by rising from the dead.

Throughout the show, Merlin is constantly playing a fool while executing amazing feats behind Arthur's back. His relationship with Arthur grows as the two slowly become best friends. Merlin is constantly saving Arthur's life while the man doesn't even know it. Can you imagine this? Day after day, week after week, year after year. Performing mighty feats of magic while no one even knows about it. Jesus actually told us three times in Matthew 6 to follow God's promptings to us behind others' backs: when we give to the needy, when we pray, and when we fast. The focus of these is not to get attention for ourselves but to experience Jesus and help others.

Eventually, Merlin does tell Arthur about his magical abilities. He takes this risk knowing Arthur has seen the terrible side of magic that is evil and focused on destruction. Merlin chooses to become an ambassador for those who use magic out of love rather than out of hatred.

We all are an ambassador for something. Some are ambassadors for very important needs like the plight of those caught in slavery or those who can't afford homes. Some, though, choose to be ambassadors for nothing more than their own selves. We call it pride. Paul explained what it means to be ambassadors for Christ in 2 Corinthians 5:11-21. We are misunderstood and sometimes unwanted. This is a role where you live not for yourself but for Christ and His mission. This leads us to selflessness, where we can fight for others even if they are confused by us.

Over the course of the last couple of seasons, we see Arthur and Merlin change the kingdom, save lives, and become the best of friends—all because Merlin was a fool who fought for others.

Quest of the Day

1. Read Hebrews 11.

2. How many of these characters at one point seemed foolish to those around them? What drove them to serve God?

3. Think of those who live in countries where religion isn't free. Imagine how the Christians feel following Christ and using spiritual gifts in a land where it is not allowed. Investigate teams like Voice of the Martyrs and other organizations that help them. How can you help join in helping them?

DAY 15 — STANLEY: ARE YOU LISTENING? BY NICK HAYDEN

For those who are led by the Spirit of God are the children of God. The Spirit you received does not make you slaves, so that you live in fear again; rather, the Spirit you received brought about your adoption to sonship. And by him we cry, "Abba, Father."

Romans 8:14-15

My favorite computer game to subject unwitting players to is *The Stanley Parable*. This is a walking simulator where you play as Stanley, a faceless worker at a nondescript office who presses the buttons his computer tells him to press until, one day (the day when you start the game), the instructions stop. The office is empty. And Stanley decides to look around and see what is going on.

As he (you) walk along the single path, the British narrator explains what Stanley is feeling, what he is seeing. Then you come to a room with two doors. And here the narrator says, "When Stanley came to a set of two open doors, he entered the door on his left."

But do you obey the narrator or not?

The rest of the game is an interaction between the player and the narrator. Do you listen or rebel? Do you try to break out of the office-complex-turned-experiment or do you wander into random corners? Do you indulge in the narrator's fancies? Do you torture him through sheer stubbornness? In a variety of clever and entertaining paths, the game examines the structure of games, the idea of free will, and other existential (and often ridiculous) quandaries—such as how long you'll wait in a broom closet to see if the narrator will continue to comment on your immobility.

But in the end, there is no real dialogue between narrator and player. The narrator dictates. The player reacts. There is antagonism between them. If you take the game in a certain way, the whole thing seems futile. Everything has been preprogrammed, and everything is a bit frivolous.

Unfortunately, this is how some view mankind's relationship with God. He dictates, and you either get in line or rebel and suffer whatever horrible designs He has planned. He is capricious, irrational, and unwilling to listen. But this is not the Bible's view of mankind's relationship with God.

For those of us who know Jesus Christ, we are indeed "narrated" to, not by a sardonic British voice actor, but by the Holy Spirit. And this leading is not dictatorial or arbitrary, but pleasant and intimate. We are not God's slaves or His playthings or His punchline. We are His children. In some remarkable way, we are sons and daughters of God just as Jesus is the Son of God. He is the example and forerunner of what we shall be.

One thing this means, and it means many things, is that we have a real relationship with the God of the universe. When Jesus taught His disciples to pray, He told them to say, "Our Father," just as He often talked of "My Father." In Romans 8:15, Paul says that the Holy Spirit enables us to cry out to God: "Abba, Father."

This is intimate. This is my son saying, "Daddy, I want to tell you something." This is my daughter asking for something special. This is not distant and cold; this is not combative. It's not Man vs. God, or player vs, narrator. It's "I will be their God, and they shall be my people" (Jeremiah 31:33).

We are not like Stanley, who is only a button-pushing cog and an existential joke, a pawn in his own game. Instead, Jesus says of us, "I have called you friends, for all that I have heard from my Father I have made known to you" (John 15:15).

Listen to the Spirit directing you, and speak to the One who made you and saved you and loves you and knows you better than you know yourself. Then you will be a walking parable of God's love.

Quest of the Day

1. Do you believe that God is involved in every aspect of your life? Practice taking a moment regularly

throughout the day (perhaps every hour on the hour) to acknowledge him and speak to him.

2. In the book of Job, Job switches seamlessly between speaking to his friends and speaking to God. Imagine a world where all Christians would flow between person-to-person dialogue and person-to-God dialogue without awkwardness or hesitation. Practice speaking to God while you do ordinary things, like washing dishes or working out.

DAY 16 - DOCTOR MORBIUS AND OUR ID
BY ERIC ANDERSON

What causes fights and quarrels among you? Don't they come from desires that battle within you?

James 4:1

What is your favorite classic 1950s film? *Forbidden Planet* is high on my list. The film features Leslie Nielson as Commander Adams, a captain of a spaceship who leads a crew that comes to check on a colony twenty years after it had landed. As they start viewing the planet from the craft and while they search for signs of life, they get radio communication from a man named Doctor Morbius (played by Walter Pidgeon), who with his daughter Altaira (played by Anne Francis), are the last survivors of that expedition. He insists that the crew should not land. He is fine and tries to push them on, but they must land to see the colony per their orders. After landing at the coordinates given to them, his robot, Robbie, comes to pick up the commander. Adams meets Morbius for lunch, and Morbius claims the others were killed off by some unseen monster, but he is happy to stay with his daughter and Robbie. He argues to kick the commander off the planet right away and calls himself a "recluse," but the crew needs to communicate with command before leaving. This means building a structure to radio home because their ship can't communicate that far with normal equipment.

As most of the crew goes to bed that night and a few stay, the camera follows a path of footprints being made by an invisible force. The guards see nothing, and when it moves something out of the way to climb into the ship, a man lying in bed looks and then goes right back to sleep, thinking it a dream. Come the morning, Commander Adams is investigating how some equipment got broken.

At a loss, he goes to see Morbius about this. He has become an archaeologist and is studying a race of creatures that is long gone. They left a huge research facility with highly advanced technology. In one of the labs, there is a device that tests your mental capabilities. It can create images of what you imagine, and Morbius has used it to train his mind. In fact, the reason they have Robbie is because of the tech and knowledge left by this long-dead civilization.

Morbius is extremely arrogant. After years of this research, he decides he is the only person who can be trusted to control when or if any of this technology or knowledge gets out to the rest of mankind. The knowledge is everything, but he does not value companionship, aside from maybe his daughter, and thinks his work is more important than anything else. He was the expert and no one else had any contributions to make.

Doctor Morbius would be a great Pharisee. When Jesus was ministering, He had a lot of arguments with them. They were arrogant and felt they did not need this man who could do miracles. They thought they should decide what people knew about God and that they held a monopoly on how to interact with Him. They had ancient knowledge, and they were fine without the Son of God. They saw no need to be rescued. In Luke 11, Jesus made a series of "woes" to Pharisees for their hypocrisy. "Then the Lord said to him, 'Now then, you Pharisees clean the outside of the cup and dish, but inside you are full of greed and wickedness'" (Luke 11:39).

In reality, the system was never meant to work without the Son of God. All the sacrifices the priests made were temporary. It was a system that kept man in constant red tape; always having to atone for this and for that. No sacrifice could change out hearts, except one, that of Jesus. As Jesus pronounced His woes, experts in the law were insulted, and Jesus stated, "And you experts in the law, woe to you, because you load people down with burdens they can hardly carry and you yourselves will not lift one finger to help them" (Luke 11:46).

The creature comes again and this time kills members of Adams's crew. Now the commander is beyond angry. Knowing that they are being kept from finding the truth, one of his officers sneaks into the lab and takes a shot at this mind machine. He discovers that the reason the aliens are gone is because of their own Ids. Their inner minds, filled with anger and deceit, had subconsciously created monsters that killed all of them. Bringing the insight to Adams and Morbius is the last thing this officer ever did. The strain of the machine is too much for his mind.

Morbius discovers that his own "Id," or his own inner mind, is responsible for the monster that killed everyone. His own selfishness came out through the machine he had used to train his mind. It created this invisible force that would attack anyone he did not trust, just as our own sin put Jesus on the cross.

How often do we think we are perfect? Do we ever check ourselves? How talented are we at cleaning the outside but leaving the inside dirty? Many of the passages in the Sermon on the Mount, found in Matthew 5-7, are portions designed to take us deeper. We say, "I have not killed anyone," but do you hate anyone? Do you handle your anger well? We say, "I don't sleep around," but do we lust after people around us or people we find on social media? I have never had sex, but I have lost battles with lust. How does your selfishness affect those around you? Do you ever try to do things alone that are meant to be done in community? Sometimes as humans we are blind to our own sin. We don't see how it affects others but just like an invisible monster, our attitude comes out. The reach of this Id monster even corrupted the trusted wildlife. A tiger that had become a "friend" to Altaira had attacked her. Fortunately, Commander Adams was there to shoot it.

Jesus warned us about this. "You have heart it said, 'Do not murder,' but that anyone who does so is subject to judgement. I tell you, anyone who is angry with his brother will be subject to judgement (Matthew 5:21-22). Yet He also took our sin upon Himself. Romans 8 tells us that in Christ we are freed from this law of sin and death and given over to the law of life.

Morbius refuses to accept help until he fully faces what he has done. He had to admit that his Id is destroying others. As he finally admits his wrong, Altaira and Robbie leave with the crew. Morbius, drowning in the sorrow of this sin, instructs Adams to push a large button. They have moments to get away from a planet that will explode.

You and I don't need to refuse help. We don't need to use the Osterhagen Key from the *Doctor Who* storyline "Journey's End." One day Jesus will make a new Earth and a new Heaven, but until then, we have this planet and, more importantly, the help of Jesus and each other.

Quest of the Day

1. Read James 4:1-10.

2. What happens when we submit in reverence to Christ?

3. Write down one or two areas you can be more submissive to Christ. Share it with someone.

DAY 17 - DINOBOT: CODE OF HERO
BY CHRIS COOKE

If we confess our sins, he is faithful and just and will forgive us our sins and purify us from all unrighteousness.

1 John 1:9

Beast Wars was my generation's *Transformers*, and in my opinion, the best version of the whole franchise. Hasbro created the toy line in the '90s to revive the *Transformers* brand, as it was all but dead, and then decided a show was to be done by Mainframe Entertainment in Canada (who were also known for *Reboot*). Why a TV series? Much like the Gen 1 Transformers line, they wanted an extended commercial for the toys. Unlike Gen 1, though, this show was done with early CGI, which severely limited its budget and character slots and forced *Beast Wars* (also known as *Beasties* on YTV in Canada) to flesh out and develop its characters a lot more than Gen 1 ever needed to. What started as a toy commercial became something that had surprising depth and fantastic characters, and debatably there is none better than the Predacon-turned-Maximal, Dinobot.

Now, our boy Dinobot, like so many of us, did not start in a good place. He is the second-in-command of the villainous Predacons, a group following Megatron, and is seen as an extremist even by his fellow Predacons. When they battle the Maximals (this gen's Autobots), their ship is damaged, and they crash onto a strange planet. Dinobot takes umbrage with Megatron's leadership, and he is quickly expelled from the Predacons. Later in that same episode, he challenges Optimus Primal for leadership of the Maximals. Optimus trips and is dangling off the ledge, but Dinobot helps him up. A confused Optimus points out that Dinobot had won. Dinobot tells him there would be no honor in such a victory, and follows it with the awesome line, "I prefer to beat my opponents the old-fashioned way...BRUTALLY!" This is the first glimpse of complexity that we get from this character, and it's a window for how we'd see his redemption.

Over the course of the first season, Dinobot adjusts to his new life as a Maximal. He often suggests the most swift, direct, and ruthless forms of attack. He challenges leadership, but he shows time and time again he can be trusted. This trust is challenged in season two. See, in the first season, Megatron is obsessed with this Golden Disk that he had stolen, and we find out it is one of two; the other being in the hands of some aliens named the Vok. Now the Vok allowed them to believe this world they'd crash-landed on was a weird testing planet with two moons, but when the characters make their move in the first season finale, we find out one of those moons is a planet-killing weapon. This set the stage for us to discover in the second season that they'd landed on prehistoric Earth. As

Dinobot learns these things, it causes him to struggle with and question many things: his loyalties, his free will, if he is destined or fated to do things, as well as feeling that if the Maximals somehow won, that he would not be accepted back on Cybertron. This causes Dinobot to briefly rejoin the Predacons, returning the Golden Disk to Megatron. The betrayal is short-lived, as he could not bring himself to kill his frenemy, Rattrap. He is then forgiven by Optimus Primal and welcomed back to the Maximals, but things are strained.

In the episode "Code of Hero," we come to not just the best episode of *Beast Wars* (and any Transformers media, fight me!), but also Dinobot's darkest and brightest hour. It begins with Dinobot on the verge of suicide (this was a kids show, by the way), but he wants to redeem himself with the Maximals, set things right, and reclaim the Disk. At the same time, Megatron discovers that they are operating by *Back to the Future* rules: what he does in Earth's past (his present) has an impact on the future. He unleashes all his forces on a valley to wipe out the proto-humans so the Autobots would lose their best ally in the Gen 1 show. Dinobot calls for backup, but it will take them a while to get there. He realizes that he has free will, but ironically he currently has no choice at all—he has to stop Megatron at all costs. He wages a brutal one-man attack on the Predacons, taking them out but suffering a lot of damage. He's at the point where his computer tries to put him in stasis lock so he can keep functioning, but he refuses, sealing his fate. As he keeps going, he knows he will die. He's outmatched by Megatron, but with luck, he knocks the Disk from his enemy's grasp, and with his last bit of power, destroys the disk. Megatron flees, and Dinobot's teammates arrive. His final words are:

> Tell my tale to those who ask. Tell it truly, the
> ill deeds along with the good, and let me be
> judged accordingly. The rest...is silence.

Dinobot's tale is quite similar to the walk and struggles we have as believers. Granted, our walk features fewer guns, dinosaurs, and time travel, but still. There are times when our convictions will be challenged, our loyalties tested in big and small ways, and where we may question and doubt. Take heart, though, brothers and sisters, as like Dinobot, but to a far greater degree, we are offered not just instruction for those times, but also forgiveness. And like Dinobot, we were born evil but have found redemption in the Lord.

Throughout the Word, we are reminded of our forgiveness and redemption in Christ. Scripture tells us:

- I have been crucified with Christ and I no longer live, but Christ lives in me. The life I now live in the body, I live by faith in the Son of God, who loved me and gave himself for me (Galatians 2:20).

- Repent, then, and turn to God, so that your sins may be wiped out, that times of refreshing may come from the Lord (Acts 3:19).

- Be kind and compassionate to one another, forgiving each other, just as in Christ God forgave you (Ephesians 4:32).

And those wonderful verses are just a quick dive. Take some time daily, especially during times of struggle (and battles with robotic T-rexes). Study the word, and take inspiration from resources that point you towards our wonderful Lord.

Quest of the Day

1. Look at whatever media you're consuming. See what parallels are there between it and your walk.

2. Ask yourself; what can you learn from it? What will you do with that learning?

3. Watch *Beast Wars*. It's a really good show.

DAY 18 – "NOT US": CAPTAIN AMERICA AND RIGHTEOUS INDIGNATION
BY NATHAN MARCHAND

When the king heard the words of the Book of the Law, he
tore his robes.

2 Kings 22:11a

On the surface, it looks like Steve Rogers (aka
Captain America) is coping with Thanos's victory in *Avengers: Endgame* pretty well, though perhaps in an unexpected way—
he has become a grief counselor. During one session, a man
says, "So I, uh... Went on a date the other day. First time in
five years, you know? Sit there, dinner.... I didn't know what
to talk about."

"What did you talk about?" Steve asks.

"Same old crap, you know? How things have
changed, and...my job, his job.... How much we miss the
Mets. Then things get quiet.... He cried as they were serving
the salads."

"How about you?"

"I cried...just before dessert. But I'm seeing him
tomorrow, so...."

"That's great. You did the hardest part. You took the
jump, you didn't know where you were gonna come down.
And that's it. That's those little brave baby steps you gotta

take. To try and become whole again. To try and find purpose. I went in the ice in forty-five right after I met the love of my life. Woke up seventy years later. You got to move on. Got to move on. The world is in our hands. It's left to us guys, and we have to do something with it. Otherwise...Thanos should have killed all of us."

In the very next scene, though, he meets a frazzled, half-blonde Natasha Romanov (aka Black Widow) in her makeshift office as she coordinates heroes across the galaxy. After some chit-chat, Steve admits that he can't take his own advice. "I keep telling everybody they should move on. Some do—but not us."

In the five years since "the Snap," Steve hasn't been able to accept their failure—his failure—to stop it. He hasn't been able to accept the fractured universe the Mad Titan left in his wake. Even Thanos's execution by Thor didn't satisfy Steve's sense of justice. That universal genocide shouldn't have happened. The misery he encountered every day because of it shouldn't exist. The man who never backed down from a bully, whether he met him in an alley or the battlefield, regretted there was one he couldn't stop.

Hence why when Scott Lang (aka Ant-Man) escapes the Microverse and tells him about his "twelve percent of a plan" to travel back in time to gather the Infinity Stones and use them to undo Thanos's handiwork, Steve leaps at the

84

chance. It's a longshot, but it's a shot. The colossal wrong could be made right.

Perhaps that's why, in one of the most epic moments I've ever seen on film, Steve was worthy to wield Mjolnir when he faced Thanos again.

In 2 Kings 22, we meet Josiah, a boy who ascended to the throne of Judah at age eight. Unlike his evil grandfather Manasseh, "[h]e did what was right in the eyes of the Lord and followed completely the ways of his father David, not turning aside to the right or to the left" (v. 2). As an adult, he sent his secretary, Shaphan, to attend to business at the temple. While there, he learned the high priest, Hilkiah, had discovered the Book of the Law, which had gone missing for decades, if not longer. Shaphan returned to the king and read from the Book. Josiah's reaction was visceral:

> When the king heard the words of the Book
> of the Law, he tore his robes. He gave these
> orders to Hilkiah the priest, Ahikam son of
> Shaphan, Akbor son of Micaiah, Shaphan the
> secretary and Asaiah the king's attendant: "Go
> and inquire of the Lord for me and for the
> people and for all Judah about what is written
> in this book that has been found. Great is the
> Lord's anger that burns against us because
> those who have gone before us have not

obeyed the words of this book; they have not

acted in accordance with all that is written

there concerning us" (2 Kings 22:11-13).

Josiah then sent Shaphan and the priests to inquire of the

prophetess Huldah concerning this. Thankfully, she said the

Lord was pleased with Josiah's humility, so Josiah wouldn't

see the disaster God would bring upon Judah.

In the following chapter, Josiah gathered his people

and read from the Book of the Covenant.

The king stood by the pillar and renewed the

covenant in the presence of the Lord—to

follow the Lord and keep his commands,

statutes and decrees with all his heart and all

his soul, thus confirming the words of the

covenant written in this book. Then all the

people pledged themselves to the covenant (2

King 23:3).

This marked the beginning of a massive reform. All the pagan

objects in the temple were removed. Idols and Asherah poles

were removed from sacred places and smashed. Mediums and

spiritists were cast out. Verse 25 tells us, "Neither before nor

after Josiah was there a king like him who turned to the Lord

as he did—with all his heart and with all his soul and with all

his strength, in accordance with all the Law of Moses."

There is much evil in the world. There has been since Adam and Eve ate that forbidden fruit. In their heart of hearts, every human who has ever lived carries the echoes of Eden. They know the world is not right, even if they don't say it. Christians, though, are fully aware of it, and our hearts burn with a righteous indignation. It's the fire that burns when we hear about things like sex trafficking. It compels us to act, to fight against the evil. This "holy discontent" makes us refuse to accept this as "normal," because it was never part of God's design, and we know this. We can't simply "move on" with our lives as if nothing happened. Just like "the Snap" drastically altered the Marvel Cinematic Universe, so the Fall of Man changed ours. Now we must take back what we lost by taking the Gospel to the ends of the Earth and through its power undo the evils of sin.

Captain America and King Josiah couldn't stand by while evil pervaded the world, and neither can we.

It's time to lift Mjolnir, my friends.

Quest of the Day

1. Read 2 Kings 22.
2. Is there a cause you've wanted to get involved in but haven't? What is it? Journal about this question.
3. Research a cause with which you could get involved (soup kitchen, mentoring, etc.) Once you've determined what that cause is, go and do it.

DAY 19 — MYSTERIO: WHAT A TANGLED WEB WE WEAVE!
BY SCOTT BAYLES

"Beware of false prophets who come disguised as harmless sheep but are really vicious wolves."

Matthew 7:15 NLT

The angsty, action-packed sequel, *Spider-Man: Far from Home*, picks up right where *Avengers: Endgame* left off and follows Peter Parker on a humorous and heartfelt European vacation. While Spidey's humble heroism never fails to inspire, it's the villain of the story who really steals the spotlight.

When four elemental monsters begin wreaking havoc all across Europe, a mysterious new hero emerges claiming, "I'm here to save your world." This courageous new hero, dubbed Mysterio by Peter and his classmates, claims to be the sole survivor of a parallel Earth. He explains to Peter that the elemental creatures first materialized on Earth 833 many years ago. "We mobilized and fought them, but with each battle they grew stronger," Mysterio recounts. "I was part of the last battalion left trying to stop them. All we did was delay the inevitable."

Having traversed the multiverse to help save Earth 616 with the help of Spider-Man, Mysterio fends off the elemental monsters at great personal risk while simultaneously forming a friendship with Peter. Believing Mysterio to be much more capable and competent than himself, Peter gives Mysterio control of EDITH: a billion-dollar tactical system embedded in a pair of sunglasses that he inherited from Tony Stark. Not surprisingly, Mysterio isn't what he seems.

To his horror, Peter discovers that Mysterio, aka Quentin Beck, isn't a hero at all. Rather, Beck turns out to be a brilliant but unbalanced ex-employee of Stark Industries. Beck utilizes advanced technology to create incredible illusions. The elemental monsters are nothing more than holographic projections and special effects. Beck desperately wants the world to believe that he is an Avengers-level hero, and he's willing to orchestrate cataclysmic disasters to accomplish his goals. With EDITH now under Beck's control, he plans another duplicitous demonstration of daring-do that will level half of London, and it's up to Spider-Man to stop him.

During a pivotal point in the movie, Mysterio snidely tells Spider-Man, "You are so gullible. I mean, you're smart as a whip, just a sucker…. It's easy to fool people when they're already fooling themselves."

While some fans may have been surprised by Mysterio's duplicitous nature, the bigger shocker came during a post-credits scene, where it's revealed that a shape-shifting Skrull had been posing as Nick Fury the entire movie. It seems

Spider-Man is surrounded by people pretending to be someone they aren't.

Mysterio reminds me a great deal of a man we read about in the Bible named Jacob. Just as Mysterio tricks Peter into handing over the tactical system he inherited from Tony Stark, Jacob once tricked his older brother, Esau, into handing over his inheritance in exchange for a bowl of soup. Making him even more like Mysterio, Jacob even went a step further by disguising himself as Esau in order to deceive their father, Isaac, into giving him the family blessing too. The Bible says, "Isaac was old and turning blind" (Genesis 27:1 NLT), so Jacob took advantage of his aging father by dressing in his brother's favorite clothes and covering his arms and the smooth part of his neck with the skin of a young goat to make himself appear more hairy like his brother. Then he brought a delicious meal to his nearly-blind father, saying, "It's Esau, your firstborn son. I've done as you told me. Here is the wild game. Now sit up and eat it so you can give me your blessing" (Genesis 27:19 NLT).

Thankfully Jacob eventually repented of his deceitful ways and became a godly man, but the world remains replete with people who pretend to be something they aren't in order to deceive others.

Jesus warned his followers, "Beware of false prophets who come disguised as harmless sheep but are really vicious wolves" (Matthew 7:15 NLT). The Apostle Paul also warned about false prophets, saying, "They are deceitful workers who disguise themselves as apostles of Christ. But I am not surprised! Even Satan disguises himself as an angel of light. So, it is no wonder that his servants also disguise themselves as servants of righteousness" (2 Corinthians 11:13-15 NLT). Satan and his servants can deceive people by appearing to be attractive, upright, and virtuous. Many unsuspecting believers have followed smooth-talking, Bible-quoting leaders into destructive heresies or dangerous cults.

During his final confrontation with Spider-Man, Mysterio quips, "People need to believe, and nowadays they'll believe anything." This is why it's important for Christians to be watchful and wary. Peter Parker learned the hard way that, as Nick Fury acknowledges, "Appearances can be deceiving." Thankfully, Mysterio's evil scheme failed and Spider-Man won in the end. We can take heart that even though deceitful schemers may fool us on occasion, God will never be fooled, and God always wins in the end.

Quest of the Day

1. Read Genesis 27:1-45.
2. What motivates people like Jacob or Quentin Beck to be deceptive? How does it benefit them?

3. How can you be on guard against wolves in sheep's clothing? How can you identify false prophets and fake people?
4. Begin now to take on discernment as a deliberate practice. Test everything you hear in light of Scripture.

DAY 20 - CHARLIE BROWN: THE LOVE OF THE FATHER
BY DARRIN BALL

I have loved you with an everlasting love.

Jeremiah 31:3

There is someone who is too embarrassed to talk to the Little Red-Haired Girl whom he has a crush on. His baseball team has never won a game. His dog gets more Valentine cards than he does. You all know his name. Of course, it's Charlie Brown.

We can all identify with Charlie Brown. We know what it's like to lose. We know what it's like for others to be more popular than we are. We know what it's like to be too shy to talk to a pretty girl or a popular guy. However, it doesn't stop there; there are so many more things that help us to identify with him. Lucy pulls the cruel trick every year of pulling the football away just as he tries to kick it. His kite gets eaten by the kite-eating tree. He gets called a "blockhead" and "wishy-washy" on a regular basis. Sometimes, it can feel a little depressing being Charlie Brown. (I take the funnies way too seriously).

But Charlie Brown never gives up. Have you ever wondered why? Every year he still runs up to kick that football. Every year he tries to fly that kite. Every year he manages that baseball team with all of its idiosyncrasies. Every day he feeds his dog, who continues to be more popular than him. All of this happens in the face of ridicule on a regular basis by the entire cast, especially by Lucy, Violet, and even his own sister, Sally.

Charlie Brown's worth is not determined by what the rest of the Peanuts gang thinks of him. (You blockhead!) I believe the secret to Charlie Brown's perseverance is revealed in one of the most popular Father's Day comic strips of all time. Charlie Brown's worth is determined by the love of his father. For those who have never read it, let me sum it up for you.

Violet is being typically ostentatious about her father. She is describing all of the things that her father is better at than Charlie Brown's father. When she gets to the fourth example, Charlie Brown interrupts her, which is something he usually does not do. "Don't say any more, come with me." He takes her to his father's barber shop. In the sixth and seventh panels, Charlie Brown says,

> See this? This is my dad's barber shop…he
> works there all day long…he has to deal with
> all sorts of people…some of them get kind of
> crabby…but you know what? I can go in there
> anytime, and no matter how busy he is, he'll

always stop, and give me a big smile…and you know why? Because he likes me, that's why!

Violet walks away downcast. After all, what could she do? How could she hope to compete with that? With all the things that her father could do, she did not truly know if her father really liked her. Charlie Brown, on the other hand, was secure in his father's affection. He knew beyond a shadow of a doubt that he could walk in there at any time and get a big smile from his dad. This was a theme that Charles Schulz made a regular part of the early strip in the 1950s and 1960s. He based it on his own father, who was a barber himself. Charles Schulz grew up knowing that his father loved him. He translated that love into his comic strip, illustrating it in the relationship between Charlie Brown and his father.

There is a confidence that comes when you know that your father loves you. You walk a little taller. You try a little harder. When someone bullies you, you don't have to respond. You don't have to prove yourself. You can walk away from a fight and know you are the better person. You don't have to have the last word in an argument. You know that there is someone who is there for you, even when you feel completely alone.

If you have faith in Jesus Christ, you are a child of God (Galatians 3:26). If you are a Christian, you have a Father who has adopted you into His own family (Romans 8:14-17). The

Apostle John marveled at what kind of love would allow us to be called children of God (I John 3:1-3). Christians have a Father who knows how to give good and perfect gifts to His children (James 1:17-18).

This also means we have a family name to live up to. Second Corinthians 6:16-18 tells us to come out from among them and be separate. Do not touch the unclean thing. Only then will God be a Father to us, and we will be His sons and daughters. There are things that God has commanded us to have nothing to do with. Even if we go astray, the parable of the prodigal son conveys to us that God will welcome us back if we repent and return to Him (Luke 15:11-32). What a loving Father!

God the Father never stops thinking about you. Psalm 139:17-18 tells us that God's thoughts about us are so great that they cannot be numbered. These thoughts that God thinks of us are precious, prized, and valuable. Isaiah 49:14-16 starts off revealing something quite sad. It states that it is possible for a woman to forget her own baby. In this sinful world, yes, that is possible. But the passage goes on to tell us that God can never forget about the ones He loves. He has inscribed our names on the palms of His hands.

Remember that those who do not have God as their Father cannot compete with that. Walk a little taller today.

Walk away from a fight. Stay away from sinfulness. *Know that God loves you as a Father. Persevere, like Charlie Brown.*

<u>Quest of the Day</u>

1. Read some comic strips. *Star Trek* and *Star Wars* nerds will enjoy *Brewster Rockit.* Fans of the vampire genre will enjoy *Scary Gary.* Then it's *Mutts* for animal lovers, *Crankshaft* for curmudgeons, and *Luann* for drama queens.

2. Read 1 John 3:1-3 and meditate on what it means to be a child of God.

3. With God as your Father, ask yourself if everything in your life measures up to His standards. Are there things with which He is not pleased? Be prepared to turn from unclean thoughts and actions.

DAY 21 — CARA DUNE: AGAINST ALL ODDS
BY SCOTT BAYLES

If God is for us, who can be against us?

Romans 8:31

The wildly popular *Star Wars* TV series *The Mandalorian* introduced audiences to a compelling, capable character named Carasynthia Dune—or, Cara for short. In an episode titled "Sanctuary," to evade capture from the bounty hunters still on his trail, the Mandolorian, aka Din Djarin, decides to land on Sorgan, a thinly-populated, out-of-the-way planet that he describes as a "real backwater skug hole." Djarin assures his little traveling companion, Grogu (better known to fans as "Baby Yoda"), "Nobody is gonna find us here."

When the duo arrives at a local tavern in search of some nourishment, Djarin meets the proud, powerful fighter Cara Dune. She reveals that she once served as a drop soldier for the Rebel Alliance, and when Mando asks what she's doing on Sorgan, she replies, "Just call it early retirement." The two warriors go their separate ways, but the Mandalorian soon learns of a small farming village being oppressed by a band of Klatooinian raiders. "Our whole harvest was stolen," one villager explains. When Djarin calls on Cara to help liberate the village and fend off the raiders, she hesitates, especially after learning the marauders possess an AT-ST, an armored imperial walker. "This is more than I signed up for," she tells Djarin. "I've seen that thing take out entire companies of soldiers in a matter of minutes…you cannot fight that thing," she warns the villagers. Although Cara feels utterly outmatched and overwhelmed, the Mandalorian won't let her walk away.

Djarin comes up with a plan to train the small band of farmers in combat and arm them with blasters. They cut down trees to build barricades and dig a deep pit to use a trap for the AT-ST. Djarin and Cara then lure the Klatooinian raiders to the village. The AT-ST advances on the village and deploys a powerful beam light, scanning the barricades. The raiders charge the fields, exchanging fire with the emboldened farmers. Cara draws the attention of the AT-ST, firing blaster bolts through its viewports. Provoked by Cara, the walker unwittingly steps into the pit and sinks into the pond. The Mandalorian charges in with a thermal detonator and plunges it through the walker's chassis, blowing it up. Deprived of their armored walker, the surviving Klatooinian raiders flee into the forest. Against all odds, Djarin and Cara, along with a ragtag bunch of farmers, defeat the raiders and celebrate their improbable victory.

Cara Dune's story is reminiscent of a reluctant hero from the Old Testament named Gideon. Much like the Klatooinian raiders who terrorized the small farming village on Sorgan, Midianite marauders oppressed the people of Israel.

The Bible says, "Whenever the Israelites planted their crops, marauders from Midian, Amalek, and the people of the east would attack Israel, camping in the land and destroying crops as far away as Gaza. They left the Israelites with nothing to eat, taking all the sheep, goats, cattle, and donkeys" (Judges 6:3-4 NLT).

Where the starving Sorganians sought help from the Mandalorian, the Israelites sought help from the Lord. The Bible says, "So Israel was reduced to starvation by the Midianites. Then the Israelites cried out to the Lord for help" (Judges 6:6 NLT). God heard the Israelites' cry and sent an angel to recruit a mighty warrior to save his people, similar to the Mandalorian recruiting Cara Dune. The Bible says, "Gideon son of Joash was threshing wheat at the bottom of a winepress to hide the grain from the Midianites. The angel of the Lord appeared to him and said, 'Mighty hero, the Lord is with you!'" (Judges 6:11-12 NLT). Like Cara, Gideon hesitated at first. He made excuses, saying, "But Lord…how can I rescue Israel? My clan is the weakest in the whole tribe of Manasseh, and I am the least in my entire family!" (Judges 6:15 NLT). Gideon felt outmatched and overwhelmed by the Midianite raiders. But God wouldn't allow Gideon to walk away. The Lord said to him, "I will be with you. And you will destroy the Midianites as if you were fighting against one man" (Judges 6:16 NLT).

It took a good deal of coaxing, but eventually Gideon mustered his courage, rallied an army of Israelites, and prepared to battle the Midianites. God ordered Gideon and his ragtag band of Israelites to surround the massive Midianite camp in the middle of the night with nothing but torches, clay pots, and ram's horns. Once they were in position, they all lit their torches, smashed their pots, and blew their horns. In one voice, the small militia chanted, "A sword for the Lord and for Gideon!" (Judge 6:20 NLT). The startled Midianite marauders were so confused and frightened, they began fighting amongst themselves and eventually fled for their lives. Gideon and his men pursued their enemies into the night and across the river until the Midianites were thoroughly vanquished. Against all odds, God gave Gideon and his small Israelite militia a mighty victory.

Even though she felt inadequate for the task, Cara Dune answered Djarin's call to fight on behalf of others and won the victory. Similarly, even though he felt inadequate for the task, Gideon answered God's call to fight for the people of Israel and won the victory. Gideon's story reminds us that, no matter the odds or how inadequate we might feel, if we respond to God's call and obey His orders, victory is not only possible, it's certain. The New Testament offers these assuring words: "If God is for us, who can be against us? ... Who shall separate us from the love of Christ? Shall trouble or hardship

or persecution or famine or nakedness or danger or sword? …
No, in all these things we are more than conquerors through
him who loved us" (Romans 8:31-37). No matter what battles
you might be fighting, the best thing you can do is trust in God
and answer His call. If God is for you, no one and nothing can
stand against you.

Quest of the Day

1. Read Judges 6 and Romans 8:31-39 in their entirety.

2. What other similarities do you see between the story of
   Cara Dune and Gideon? Differences?

3. Both Cara and Gideon fought battles on behalf of
   others who were being bullied and oppressed. What
   battles might God be calling you to fight on behalf of
   others?

4. If you know of someone who is struggling, take a
   moment today to ask them how you can help.

DAY 22 - WESTLEY'S PRAYER TO THE LORD OF PERMANENT AFFECTION
BY DARRIN BALL

In the day of trouble I call upon You, for You answer me.

Psalm 86:7 (ESV)

Nathan Marchand and I have a disagreement, and I need your help. We were talking about that old cliché, "The book is always better." He mentioned that there are a couple of exceptions to this rule. When he said, "*The Princess Bride,*" I almost got up out of my chair. Then he said that the movie and the book were equals, that one could not be put above the other, and I sat back down.

I couldn't understand how the book could be better until I read it for myself. *The Princess Bride* seems like the perfect movie. But the book by William Goldman (who presents an abridgement of Morgenstern's classic tale) is better. Interesting fact: William Goldman also wrote the screenplay for his own book, which is why Nathan believes the movie to be exceptional.

But the story of how Buttercup and Westley discover they truly love each other is better in the book, just as the Zoo of Death is better than the Pit of Despair. In the second chapter, Prince Humperdinck is there wrestling with an orangutan. He snaps its spine, and it falls like a ragdoll. The

103

lowest level of the Zoo of Death is the fifth level, which is kept empty as Humperdinck hopes to find something as dangerous and powerful as he is.

The story of Domingo Montoya is fascinating. This completely unknown sword maker is the pawn of Yeste to make the most brilliant swords when Yeste knows he is out of his league. The rise of Inigo to the rank of one higher than master in swordsmanship (wizard) is captivating. And the rhyming of Fezzik is mainly in his head. It is a tool to help him think. Buttercup's first nightmare (Boo!) is tame compared to the terrors that followed. In every way, the book is better.

Did you know that the resurrection pill from Miracle Max was only supposed to last for 60 minutes? This is why they waited to give him the pill until they were on top of the wall. But wait, Miracle Max remembers later that he made a mistake. He adds the wrong amount of one ingredient, so the resurrection pill would only last for 40 minutes. What would happen to Westley after the 60 (or 40) minutes? Not sure. He might have collapsed again and needed tending for up to a year to heal properly.

This is why Inigo calculates the timing of how long it would take to get inside the castle, avenge his father, get Buttercup, and get out. They were operating under the premise that they only had 60 minutes. As the events of "storming the castle" unfold, Morgenstern (in the story within a story) is counting down the time. "The time was then 5:27." That is when we hear the word "Mawidge." "It was now 5:37." That is when Count Rugan turns and runs. Westley assumes he has until 6:15. Actually, he only has until 5:55, but how could he know? At exactly 5:48, he stops Buttercup from committing suicide with a Florinese dagger. He only has seven minutes until the effects of the resurrection pill wear off.

At 5:52 is when Westley reveals that he is the Dread Pirate Roberts to Prince Humperdinck. He explains "to the pain" to someone who has inflicted pain on numerous creatures over the years, killing them with all manner of weapons. When Westley commands, "Drop your sword!" Humperdinck obeys. And then at exactly 5:55, Westley's eyes roll into his head, and his body crumples. The man who could snap the spine of a simian saw this moment of weakness and went to grab his sword. But suddenly, miraculously, Westley opens his eyes and shouts, "To the pain!" Humperdinck cowardly sits back down.

Later, as they are escaping on horses, Buttercup asks Westley if he is all right. She mentions how she was worried when his eyes rolled up. Westley explains, "I suppose I was dying again, so I asked the Lord of Permanent Affection for the strength to live the day. Clearly, the answer came in the affirmative." The rescue of Buttercup and happily ever after came because of answered prayer.

Have you ever come to the end of your strength? If so, you can relate to our hero, Westley. Throughout the story, Westley had accomplished mighty feats, especially surviving the fire swamp. But at 5:55, Westley was weak, frail, and one hair's breadth from death. He cries out, and the Lord answers him.

Another warrior cried out to God after having accomplished mighty feats (Judges 15:9-20). Samson snapped the ropes that bound him like they were melted wax. He had no weapon, so he grabbed a jawbone of a donkey. He single-handedly killed over a thousand Philistine warriors. But for all his might, he could not find water in the middle of the desert. Completely fatigued, he would have died of thirst after his victory. Samson knew that the same God who provided strength could also provide water in the desert. The spring of water gushed forth because he called out to God. He named it *En-hakkore,* which means "the Spring of the Caller."

When do you pray? Do you wait for a crisis? If you do, that's completely fine. God is not holding it against you that you did not start praying sooner. I think that some people have this impression of God that He is likened to a jealous overlord who might say, "Oh, so *now* you come calling out to me. You haven't talked to me in three days and now you're in trouble, and you think I should just snap my fingers and pay attention to you?" God loves to hear from us, no matter the occasion.

Because of the sacrifice of Jesus Christ on the cross, we have an open invitation to come to the throne of grace (Hebrews 4:16; 10:19-20).

Here are some of the occasions that the Bible tells us to pray.

- Is anyone suffering? James 5:13 ~ It's time to pray.
- Is anyone sick? James 5:14 ~ It's time to pray.
- Is anyone anxious? Philippians 4:6 ~ It's time to pray.
- Is the devil stalking you? 1 Peter 5:7-8 ~ It's time to pray.
- Is it a day of trouble? Psalm 50:15 ~ It's time to pray.

Are you sensing a theme? *Any trouble you might encounter, it's time to pray.* When that crisis hits, God wants you to call out to him. When you are at the end of your strength, when you have exhausted yourself from battle, when there is no way out, when death comes calling, ask the Lord of Permanent Affection for the strength to live the day.

Quest of the Day

1. Buy the book *The Princess Bride*. Read it. Then write a letter to Nathan Marchand and tell him the truth. Make sure and send it through the postal service.
2. Spend time praying over the crisis events in your personal world.
3. Spend time praying for the crisis events in our entire world.

DAY 23 - HARUO SAKAKI: CHOOSE TO LOSE THE BATTLE
BY NATHAN MARCHAND

For whoever wants to save his life will lose it, but whoever loses his life for me will find it.

Matthew 16:25

Haruo Sakaki's single-minded obsession is rivaled only by Captain Ahab. Indeed, throughout the (in)famous Godzilla anime trilogy—*Godzilla: Planet of the Monsters, Godzilla: City on the Edge of Battle,* and *Godzilla: The Planet Eater*—the titular kaiju (giant monster) is his "white whale." The monster's assault on Earth forced a remnant of humanity and a few aliens to escape into space to find a new home and left Haruo an orphan. In the following years, the young man's grief morphed into rage.

Low on supplies and unable to find a home, the refugees return to Earth in desperation. But thanks to the physics of faster-than-light travel (thanks, Einstein), they arrive after 20,000 years has passed. The world has been reshaped to Godzilla's liking. It's then that Haruo's rage-fueled obsession is unleashed. He leads two attacks on the kaiju, both of which fail. People die. His would-be girlfriend, Yuko, is infected with nanometal and put into a coma. He's manipulated by the cult leader Metphies to use Haruo's burning anger to usher the three-headed interdimensional dragon King Ghidorah into their universe. It's only then that Haruo sees what his rage is doing that he throws it aside for the greater good.

In the following years, Haruo settles down with Maina, a woman from the Houtua, a tribe that worships the insect kaiju Mothra. A human scientist has discovered how to reactivate an old battlemech suit, which he says will lead to the re-establishment of technology and human civilization. Haruo, knowing that this along with his lingering rage toward Godzilla will pave the way for Ghidorah to return, wrestles with a difficult decision. He must face Godzilla again, alone.

"If you go, you'll lose," Maina tells him.

"You're right," Haruo replies. "But if life is only about winning, we're the same as beasts. But what makes us human is if we need to, we can choose to lose the battle."

With the nanometal-laden body of Yuko in hand, Haruo flies the mech at Godzilla. Seconds before the monster destroys it, Haruo finally finds peace and smiles. With no technology to make war and no anger to open the interdimensional gate, Earth is safe from Ghidorah.

While this trilogy has earned the ire of many Godzilla fans, I see a deeply spiritual and redemptive story. The words Haruo speaks to Maina encapsulate one of the trilogy's key themes. While I compared him to Captain Ahab, unlike Ahab Haruo is able to see what the dire consequences of his rage— even the far-reaching ones—will be. This leads him to make a noble sacrifice that will save both his fellow humans and the Houtua. But in order to do that, he must "choose to lose." He must fight a losing battle and lay down his life.

Jesus famously said something similar to his disciples: Whoever wants to be my disciple must deny himself and take up his cross and follow me. For whoever wants to save his life will lose it, but whoever loses his life for me will find it. What good will it be for a man if he gains the whole world, yet forfeits his soul? Or what can a man give in exchange for his soul? (Matthew 16:24-26)

In other words, following Christ may result in the loss of physical life, but the follower will save his spiritual life. This saying of Jesus's is recorded in all four Gospels (twice in two of them!) Clearly, it was something very important to Him. It's paradoxical, though. "Lose your life to find it." Maina and her people in the anime trilogy are all about preserving life and avoiding death. The concept of choosing to die for the greater good is beyond strange to them. The same can be said of most people when it comes to this teaching. Following Jesus demands everything from us. He will settle for nothing less.

Will you choose to lose?

<u>Quest of the Day</u>

1. Read Matthew 16:21-28.

110

2. Journal about some obsessions you have that have distracted you from serving Jesus to your fullest potential. Write them in a list.

3. Choose an item from this list. If it's nothing sinful, fast from it for a few days (or perhaps a week). Something like video games or YouTube. If it is a sin, seek accountability to break that cycle of sin this week.

DAY 24: SAINT WALKER
BY ERIC ANDERSON

But hope that is seen is no hope at all. Who hopes for what they already have? But if we hope we wait for it patiently.

Romans 8:24-25

Bro'dee Walker's story does not start in a situation about which you would feel hopeful. He is on a pilgrimage to a mountain-top where a prophecy has told there will be a prophet someday to bring hope to his planet, Astonia. This journey is perilous, and one by one, his family keeps dying, victims, with many others, of the accidents while trying to escape violence incited by the fear of a dying sun. In all of this craziness, he does not lose hope even once. He firmly believes that "all will be well." In his conviction, he manages to rally his planet together with his message of hope. Inspired by his hope, two of the Guardians of the Universe, a group known for creating the Green Lantern Corps, replenish the dying star Astonia orbits and offer him something never seen before: a Blue Lantern Ring.

While the Green Lanterns are centered on willpower, the Blue Lanterns are capable of great hope, always trusting that the light at the end of the proverbial tunnel is there. We first meet Saint Walker in *Green Lantern* Volume 4 #25 from 2007, written by Geoff Johns. Hal Jordan is injured, and

Walker uses his Power Ring to heal him. The Blue Lanterns have a very different power than the Green Lanterns. They are more of a support unit capable both of calming some of the other Lanterns down or empowering them further.

There are seven different Lantern Corps: green {will}, red {rage}, blue {hope}, orange {avarice}, indigo {compassion}, and violet {love}, plus Black Lanterns {death} and two White Lanterns {life}. All the corps have their own oaths. Here is the Blue Lantern Oath:

> In fearful day, in raging night, with strong hearts full our souls ignite.
> When all seems lost in the war of light, look to the stars for hope burns bright!

During the Black Lantern saga, corps unite in a raging battle against the Black Lanterns. Larfleeze, the Orange Lantern of Avarice, dodges in and out and around Lanterns taking their shots, getting in the way, and risking their lives. Walker flies up to him with full hope that he can be a productive part of the team. Due to Walker's influence, Larfleeze calms down, stays centered, and helps the other corps with the fight.

In episode 13 of *Green Lantern: The Animated Series*, we find a GL named Killowog in space facing an entire armada of Red Lantern ships. He is no wimp, but an armada is not fun to face alone. Saint Walker flies in, giving him a power boost and disabling a ship with a punch. He also brought a friend: a planet called Mogo. The planet itself is a Green Lantern. Mogo blasts a huge bolt of GL energy through Walker, who then allows it to flow through him and magnifies it, thereby disabling all the ships in one blast.

Saint Walker is not glib in his hope. In *Green Lantern* Volume 4 #48, we find him sitting with Atrocitus, the fearsome leader of the Red Lanterns:

Walker: Your rage subsides on the very spot it was born.

Atrocitus: Do not pretend to understand me, Saint Walker.

Walker: I lost my family on a pilgrimage to save my planet. I cursed my god and this universe. I was enraged, too.

Having hope does not mean you easily overcome various fears or rage. It does not ignore how bad circumstances have become. In fact, Saint Walker knows hope because he has been through tragedy. In Psalm 9:18, David wrote, "The hope of the afflicted will never perish." That is not the hope of the content, or the hope of the happy, or the hope of the glib; it is the hope of those who are "afflicted." If I have a chocolate chip cookie in front of me, I don't hope for one; I eat it! Then in the absolute terror that all the cookies are gone, I hope for more. So, what does hope look like?

And we boast in the hope of the glory of God.
Not only so, but we also glory in our sufferings,
because we know that suffering produces
perseverance; perseverance character; and
character hope. And hope does not put us to
shame, because God's love has poured out into
our hearts through the Holy Spirit, who has
been given to us (Romans 5:2b-5).

Hope is born in the middle of suffering and out of perseverance. Hope is treated as an emotion in the Lantern mythos, but in reality it is far more than an emotion: hope is a verb. You don't just have hope, you do hope. You don't just want hope, you choose to hope.

Each of the moments form Saint Walker's life I have mentioned connect with different forms of feeling hopeless. Loss of loved ones. Fear of natural disaster. Getting caught in our own destructive emotions. Facing enormous odds that we cannot overcome even if no one tells us those odds. These can all affect our ability to hope, but this hope is not meant for an easy life.

In Gethsemane, Jesus felt this mix of feelings as He approached His death. He told His three closest disciples, "My soul is overwhelmed with sorrow to the point of death. Stay here and keep watch with me" (Matthew 26-38). He knew what was coming. He knew that it included being beaten, mocked, and hung on a cross. But He still faced it. When Jesus stopped his disciples from protecting Him with the sword, He told them it could have been avoided. "Do you think I cannot call on my Father, and he will at once put at my disposal more than twelve legions of angels? But how then would the Scriptures be fulfilled that say it must happen in this way?" Jesus saw a future with redemption. He saw the outcome of the pain He was going to partake in. His hope was not in escaping the difficulty but seeing what laid on the other side.

There is a lie that says hope must feel amazing. It doesn't always feel good. Sometimes hope is incredibly difficult and comes in the form of resilience. When Saint Walker kept going on his pilgrimage, the hope did not take away the pain. It didn't make him feel wonderful. He was enraged. But he trusted in the knowledge that a prophecy would be kept. He looked for the outcome rather than the surroundings.

The interesting thing about this prophecy is that he fulfilled it himself. He went looking for someone else only to find that he needs to step into the prophecy rather than watch it. When introducing himself to Killowog in the cartoon, he says, "I am merely a conduit of the great hope that surrounds us all." Jesus is the ultimate conduit, but He has called us to be miniature conduits running off of Him. Read John 15 and you will learn that we are the branches and He is the vine. In the world of grapes, they come off of branches that come off a huge vine. Jesus encouraged us to "remain" in Him as He "remains" in us. We have not just the freedom to pull our strength and hope from Him, but His admonition to do so. "Remain in me" was not a nice idea; it was a command. He wants us to be part of the redemption strategy, part of the action, part of the solution. His hope is our hope, and we are expected to give it to others.

So, how do we give others hope? It might be walking up to someone who is upset and asking what is wrong. It could be sitting with someone who always sits alone or helping your neighbor clean up after a storm. Sometimes hope comes through a conflict by challenging a friend to grow. John the Baptist told people if you have extra clothes, share with those who don't, and if you have extra food, do the same. For many people recently, hope has included going to protests, social distancing, and finding ways to occupy kids at home. Please know that hope does not attack. You should always use your freedom of speech to help or challenge but never to harm.

Jesus started his ministry by reading a passage from Isaiah, and it certainly fits as a Lantern oath:

> "The Spirit of the Lord is on me because He
> has anointed me to preach good news to the
> poor. He has sent me to proclaim freedom for
> the prisoners and recovery of sight for the

blind, to set the oppressed free, to proclaim the year of the Lord's favor" (Isaiah 61:1-2).

Quest of the Day

1. Read Hebrews 10:19-38.
2. Make two columns and write down difficulties and reasons to persevere.
3. Actively take opportunities to spread hope.

DAY 25 – THE UNMATCHED MEDUSA AND THE GORGON'S HEART
BY NICK HAYDEN

And I will give you a new heart, and a new spirit I will put within you. And I will remove the heart of stone from your flesh and give you a heart of flesh. And I will put my Spirit within you, and cause you to walk in my statutes and be careful to obey my rules.

Ezekiel 36:26-27

The one thing everyone knows about Medusa is that her look turns men to stone. Her hideous visage and head of writhing vipers don't only curdle stomachs, they solidify flesh. Yet I am not aware of anyone who has tried to capture in writing that last moment when a tragic soul looks into her monstrous eyes. Do they see forever that horrible, disfigured face? Are their lifeless dreams filled with the sinuous motions of dozens of venomous snakes? Do they forever regret the will that brought them to look into the Gorgon's eyes? (Perhaps an Unmatched player who's been on the receiving end of her attacks can answer my questions).

Whatever their final thought, they are forever after changed to stone. A statue does not move. It does not act. It does not live. It is forever captive to that moment in which it was petrified.

119

In the same way, our sin—no matter what regret we may have, what guilt we may feel—is evidence of our own petrified hearts.

One of the great promises of the Old Testament, though, is that God would remove our hearts of stone and replace them with hearts of flesh. We are not Perseus, the hero, come to slay the monster. We have already been conquered. We have already looked into the horrifying and fleetingly pleasant face of sin and have been caught. We are as good as dead, unable to move toward God, unable to act in response to his kindness.

There is a reason that in *The Lion, the Witch, and the Wardrobe*, the White Witch's courtyard is filled with statues. She is another type of Medusa, enslaving creatures by her power. And Aslan, Narnia's Christ-figure, by his breath, grants them life again.

God grants the same life to us. It is through the Cross and by the Holy Spirit that we are reawakened from our slumber, that we are made free to know God and to love him, that we are given "life and have it abundantly" (John 10:10).

Now that we have been made flesh again, now that we have escaped Medusa's collection, we can now, like Perseus, fight against her stultifying gaze. Just as Perseus uses a mirrored shield to approach and slay the monster, James encourages

Christians to look "into the perfect law, the law of liberty" and so put into action the Gospel that saved us (James 1:25).

We are no longer incapacitated, unable to obey. We have been given life, we have been made flesh, so let us be active in our faith. Let us put into actions our love toward one another. We are no longer hard-hearted, so let us not resist doing as we know we should. The Spirit of God is with us, animating us, away from the realm of Medusa and death, and into the world of Spirit-filled flesh.

Quest of the Day:

1. Do you feel hard-hearted toward God? Are there things you know you should do but feel incapable of doing? Tell him. Pray for his Spirit to invigorate you and move you to obedience.

2. Consider your life as a Christian. In what ways have you grown in obedience and love? Thank God for these things. These are evidences of your heart of flesh.

3. Paul writes, "As for you, brothers, do not grow weary in doing good" (2 Thessalonians 3:13). Find a verse that encourages you to follow God whole-heartedly. Put it in a place you will see regularly.

DAY 26 – TOMMY OLIVER: GREEN WITH EVIL! BY SCOTT BAYLES

Whoever turns a sinner from the error of their way will save them from death and cover over a multitude of sins.

James 5:20

The cult-classic *Mighty Morphin' Power Rangers* television series first aired on Fox Kids way back in 1993. While the highly-successful show spawned countless spin-offs and movies, the original series certainly set the standard.

Following the accidental release of the long-imprisoned evil space-sorceress Rita Repulsa, a benevolent sage known as Zordon recruits a team of "teenagers with attitude" to help protect Angel Grove from the wicked witch and her horde of monsters. The five teens chosen are Jason the Red Ranger, Kimberly the Pink Ranger, Billy the Blue Ranger, Zack the Black Ranger, and Trini the Yellow Ranger. Zordon grants these teenagers the ability to morph into a fighting force known as the Power Rangers, providing them with an arsenal of weapons, as well as colossal assault machines called Zords, which can combine into a giant mecha known as the Megazord.

As a twelve-year-old, I immediately fell in love with this zany, over-the-top action series and desperately wanted to be the Red Ranger when I grew up. My eventual favorite character, though, didn't join the cast until part way through the first season. In a five-episode story arc titled "Green with Evil," the show's creators introduced Tommy Oliver the Green Ranger.

As a new student at Angel Grove High School with martial arts skills that rival even Jason's, Tommy catches the eye of the evil empress Rita Repulsa. Rita sends her lackeys, the Putties, to kidnap Tommy and bring him to her lair on the moon. There, she places a spell over Tommy and transforms him into the evil Green Ranger dedicated to the destruction of the Power Rangers.

After infiltrating and ransacking the team's Command Center, the Green Ranger bests the other Rangers in battle, sending them in retreat back to their damaged headquarters. Eventually, the Power Rangers regroup and defeat the evil Green Ranger in battle and destroy his Sword of Darkness, breaking Rita's spell.

While Tommy lays defeated in the sand, Jason rushes to his side. "Are you okay, Tommy?" Jason asks.

"What happened to me?" Jason mutters in response.

"You're no longer under Rita's power," Jason assures his fallen foe.

Finally coming to his senses, Tommy penitently wonders aloud, "What have I done?"

"What you did, you did under Rita's influence," Jason responds. "You own the power now. Fight by our side, and we can defeat Rita."

"After everything that's happened?" Tommy says doubtfully.

"Tommy, we need you. It's where you belong," Jason assures his fellow Ranger.

Then, extending a friendly hand, Jason asks, "Will you join us, Tommy?"

With a nod and a handshake, Tommy's life changes course.

Back at the Command Center, Zordon proclaims, "Finally the prophecy has been fulfilled! The sixth Ranger is now one of us!"

Together, the six Power Rangers work together to foil Rita Repulsa's evil plans and save the citizens of Angel Grove.

I can't help but notice some spiritual parallels in Tommy's tale.

Rita's evil influence clouded Tommy's mind and corrupted his morals. Sin has a similar effect on us. The Bible describes sin's influence, saying,

> Their minds are full of darkness; they wander
> far from the life God gives because they have
> closed their minds and hardened their hearts
> against him. They have no sense of shame.

They live for lustful pleasure and eagerly practice every kind of impurity (Ephesians 4:18-19 NLT).

Apart from Christ, sin closes our minds and corrupts our morals. While under sin's spell, we become enemies of God. Sin leads us down a dark and destructive path away from God's goodness and grace. Without faith in Jesus, unbelievers have no hope of breaking sin's spell. But even believers wrestle with sin and sometimes surrender to its seductive influence. Thankfully, though, we are not alone in our battle.

Just as the other Power Rangers reached out to Tommy, confronting him and helping him to overcome Rita's grasp, close Christian friends can do the same for us. The Bible says, "My dear brothers and sisters, if someone among you wanders away from the truth and is brought back, you can be sure that whoever brings the sinner back from wandering will save that person from death and bring about the forgiveness of many sins" (James 5:20 NLT). As Christians, we're called to do for one another what Jason and the other Rangers did for Tommy. It's our responsibility as brothers and sisters in Christ to watch out for each other, to keep one another accountable, and help each other conquer the sins that beset us. By reaching out to unbelievers and wayward Christians, we can help them turn from a life of sin and restore them to God's favor and fellowship. Through the encouragement and help of close

Christian friends, we can foil Satan's evil schemes and experience true victory in Jesus.

<u>Quest of the Day</u>

1. Read Ephesians 4:17-24.

2. How is sin like an evil spell? How is it different?

3. Can you think of someone who has allowed sin to lead them away from God? If someone comes to mind, reach out to that person and help him or her experience forgiveness and restoration.

DAY 27 – NO-FACE: GIMME IT
BY NICK HAYDEN

Their end is destruction, their god is their belly, and they
glory in their shame, with minds set on earthly things.

Phillipians 3:19

Spirited Away was the first film by famed animator
Hayao Miyazaki I saw in the theater. It was a wild, strange
journey for this newbie to anime. My senses were
overwhelmed with surprising, evocative images: parents-
turned-pigs, a spirit bathhouse, a boy who is also a dragon, a
giant baby, a great-nosed witch, a dirty river spirit, and,
especially, No-Face.

No-Face creeped me out the first time I watched the
movie. He's a black, vaguely ghost-like spirit with a white mask.
He doesn't speak, but he tries to bargain with the other
characters. He wants to give them what they want. In this
bathhouse, what people want is gold.

So, he gives them gold, and they give him food. He
becomes a monstrous, gluttonous being, wanting more, giving
the spirits more of what they want and consuming, consuming.
He is emptiness, wanting more, needing more, and willing to
pay for it.

And yet, after our heroine Chihiro reduces him down
to size (literally), No-Face shows a different side. An empty

being, he becomes the companion of the witch Zeniba, who lives simply in a cottage far from civilization. Here, No-Face begins to work with his hands. He learns to knit and sew. He is no longer consuming, but creating.

Watching *Spirited Away*, I can't help but think of two contrasting Bible verses. First, Philippians 3:19: "Their end is destruction, their god is their belly, and they glory in their shame, with minds set on earthly things." This is No-Face at the center of the movie. He wants—he wants to "be" what others need him to be. He wants to give gold, to eat what they give him, to run insatiably after the next earthly thing. He is ruled by his desires, and those desires are unanchored from meaning and purpose.

Without God, this is man. We need to fill the emptiness somehow. Maybe we glut ourselves on work or entertainment, politics or food, outrage or romance. Our god is our stomach; our appetite for the next kick of adrenaline masters us.

Those who know Christ, though, are different. We know the only thing that can fill the emptiness is God Himself. Once that happens, once we are made truly alive by the Spirit of God, we respond in a new way. Paul says in 1 Thessalonians 4:10b-11: "But we urge you, brothers, to [love one another], and to aspire to live quietly, and to mind your own affairs, and to work with your hands...."

Freed from our need to consume, we become quiet, peaceable creators. With our hearts healed, we can use our hands to do God's work. Paul seems to say Christians should be marked by a lack of restless striving. Instead, we are known for not needing what everyone else demands—whether attention or excitement or stuff.

This does not seem flashy or revolutionary, but it is. It's a revolution from the inside out. That's the only revolution that remains in the end. We are not No-Faces, desperate to define ourselves by the material of this world, by bargains and consumption, and in the process becoming monstrous. We are Christians—we "put on the Lord Jesus Christ" (we don't wear a mask, but Christ) "and make no provision for the flesh, to gratify its desires" (Romans 13:14).

Only then can we truly live and create and love one another.

Quest of the Day

1. What "appetite" most motivates you? What worldly thing or pleasure do you chase after? (It can be something unique to yourself.) Be honest. We all chase after something. Recognizing it allows you to give it to Jesus. Do that now.

2. What does it mean, do you think, "to aspire to live quietly, and to mind your own affairs, and to work with your hands" in your context? What would that look like

in your own life? What might it mean giving up? Write a letter to God telling him what you think it might mean and asking him to respond.

DAY 28 - FACE THE DAY LIKE MOON KNIGHT
BY CHRIS COOKE

Finally, be strong in the Lord and in his mighty power. Put
on the full armor of God, so that you can take your stand
against the devil's schemes.

Ephesians 6:10-11

All right homies, first things first. Moon Knight is *not*
"Marvel's Batman." They're both rich (Moon Knight might be
a millionaire, but that's not close to Wayne's billionaire status),
they fight crime, they use gadgets, and that's where the
similarities end. The main difference is Moon Knight at one
point did have superpowers and is the avatar of the Egyptian
moon god, Khonshu, with whom he has had a strained
relationship. Another standout difference is that Moon Knight
has Dissociative Identity Disorder (formerly called Multiple
Personality Disorder). Many superheroes have aliases or roles
they assume, but Moon Knight legitimately becomes other
personalities, which he can get lost in entirely. This has been
one of the most interesting facets of Moon Knight's character
and has become a great way for the comic medium to explore
mental health issues. Let's look at the different personalities,
shall we?

First, we have Moon Knight's main personality: Marc
Spector, former boxer, ex-CIA agent, and mercenary. The next

131

is Steven Grant, a millionaire persona he uses to rub elbows with the elite and separate himself from his past. The third is Jake Lockley, a cab driver who is used to keeping his ear to the ground and remaining in contact with street and criminal elements. As I mentioned, these aren't just aliases he takes; they are people he becomes. Each serves a purpose and fulfills a function. Perhaps my favorite display of this comes from issue #8 of Moon Knight's 2014 run.

So, as a kidnapping begins and news spreads, we meet our vengeful hero scaling the side of the Freedom Tower, in contact with NYPD detective Flint. As he's breaching the tower's 54th floor, he notifies detective Flint that, "Mr. Knight" (an alias he uses while working directly with the NYPD) has the night off and to call him Grant. Moon Knight then quietly gets close to the hostages and sees the terrorist with the bombs. As he relays information and images to Detective Flint, he loses his cape, dismisses Grant, and tells himself, "Lockley, you're up." He then dons a different face cover and some armor to do the dirty work of taking down the terrorist (rather brutally, I'll add) and freeing the hostages. Moon Knight then contacts Detective Flint, becoming Mr. Knight once more as he is leaving the scene.

So, how does this relate to us in our day-to-day lives? In all honesty, the first time I read this issue, it reminded me of putting on the Armor of God. In his letter to the Christians in Ephesus, Paul instructs,

> Put on the whole armor of God, that you may be able to stand against the schemes of the devil. For we do not wrestle against flesh and blood, but against the rulers, against the authorities, against the cosmic powers over this present darkness, against the spiritual forces of evil in the heavenly places. Therefore take up the whole armor of God, that you may be able to withstand in the evil day, and having done all, to stand firm (Ephesians 6:10-14).

To face the issues at hand, Moon Knight was ready at each stage. He was prepared for each situation, and if he wasn't, he became someone who was. As believers, this is what we need to do to face the day and all the trials, struggles, temptations, and anything else that's gonna come our way. Now unlike our boy Moon Knight, we don't need to scale buildings or dislocate shoulders to do this, but we do need to put on our new selves, turn to the Lord (and our brothers and sisters in Christ) daily, and continue to become who He is transforming us into. Some days will be harder than others, but we still prepare, and know the Lord will get us through it.

Let's hit the armory, homies.

Quest of the Day

1. Write down things you struggle with that can pop up throughout your day.

2. Prayerfully approach a brother or sister who can support you in whatever way you need.

3. Bookmark Ephesians 6:10-18 to flip to for easy access and reminder whenever needed.

4. Track and mark your progress.

5. Celebrate the Lord's growth in you.

DAY 29 - CLARA'S DEMANDS (OR HOW TO TAKE THE WRONG ATTITUDE) BY ERIC ANDERSON

Who may ascend into the hill of the Lord? And who may stand in His holy place? He who has clean hands and a pure heart, who has not lifted up his soul to falsehood and has not sworn deceitfully.

Psalm 24:3-4

Clara Oswald, played by Jenna Coleman, is numb, but she is also angry and upset. She had been on the phone with her boyfriend, Danny Pink, when it became silent. Then someone else spoke to her. Danny had been hit by a car. He was dead. Not killed by a Cyberman or a Dalek or swallowed up by a black hole. He was hit by a car. What would you do? What lengths would you go to in your grief and desire to get a loved one back from the dead? As a Companion to Peter Capaldi's Doctor, she has a few more options than you or me. She is the "impossible girl." In order to stop the Great Intelligence from destroying the Doctor by polluting his timeline, she had walked into the timeline and helped him throughout his lives. She even checked in on the First Doctor to make sure he took the right Tardis. She was almost killed by doing it and was only saved because the Doctor did something crazy to get her out of the timeline. He owes her, or at least that is how she sees it.

We find her in season 8 episode 11, "Dark Water." She doesn't exactly walk in and ask for help. She comes into the Tardis asking for a sleep patch, then slowly gathers the keys to the Tardis from this spot, that spot, and well, that spot over there. These are not normal keys. These keys are almost indestructible and grant access to the most powerful contraption in the known universe, the TARDIS (Time and Relative Dimension in Space). She also puts a sleep patch on the Doctor's neck, knocking him out, or so she thinks.

When the Doctor "wakes up," they are on a volcanic planet on a spot of rock, and she is ready to throw the keys into the lava if he doesn't take her back to save Danny. She shows him the keys and throws one in the lava. But he keeps saying, "No." She keeps throwing the keys in the lava, trying to force his hand. He still refuses because taking her back in her own timeline would cause a paradox. Finally, after throwing the last one, she falls down, sobbing. Now she isn't just angry at how her boyfriend died, or that he died while she was on the phone with him trying to confess about keeping secrets. She is now angry at herself for trying to force the Doctor's hand and willfully destroying important keys for the TARDIS. She has betrayed the Doctor. She has tried to force him to do a big deed instead of simply asking him for help.

What is it you want in life? A house? A successful career? A spouse? What have you lost? Jobs? Friends? Roommates? If something vastly important is taken from you or if you don't have what you want, what lengths will you go to in order to get it? Clara went so far as to betray someone and threaten him and willfully destroy his property. She was trying to force someone more powerful to do the impossible for her. I remember someone I knew was once angry that he did not have a ministry position. He was trying to demand it from God. How do you think God felt about that?

Job was a man who lost everything. His children, flocks, servants. Even his health. All because God and the devil had a wager. The devil claimed that if God took everything away, Job would no longer worship him. So God, banking on Job being faithful, gave Satan limited permission to bring harm to Job. He took everything except his wife and his life. Job did not try to demand anything, but he did get bad advice. His friends said he must have sinned. He must have done something egregious against God. His wife wasn't any better and told him to "curse God and die." Job questioned God. He demanded answers for why this was happening. God chose to speak to him out of a storm:

> Who is this that obscures my plans with words
> without knowledge? Brace yourself like a man;
> I will question you, and you shall answer me.

Where were you when I laid the earth's foundation? Tell me, if you understand. Who marked off its dimensions? Surely you know! Who stretched a measuring line across it? ...Have you ever given orders to the morning or shown the dawn its place, that it might take the earth by its edges and shake the wicked out of it? (Job 38:2-5, 12-13).

Job has a simple answer:

I am unworthy—how can I reply to you? I put my hand over my mouth. I spoke once but have no answer—twice but I will say no more (Job 40:4-5).

We often go to God in prayer. This is done in church and in private; in homes, forests, while driving, etc. God is not unloving and unconcerned about your needs. But He is GOD. We should always approach Him with respect. When Jesus taught His disciples about prayer, He gave us a prayer that is often called the "Lord's Prayer" or the "Our Father." The very first thing we are to pray: "Our Father, hallowed be your name." Our point of prayer should always begin with respect and recognition of Whom we are praying to. This is the God who created the seas and developed systems such as DNA, the Water Cycle, and the human cell. Neither you nor I can force Him to do anything, nor should we even consider it. But take heart, for this God of ours is not silent or indifferent. He is the King of Kings, but He is also Immanuel, which means "God with us." He is the Lion, but He is also the Lamb.

Do you know what the Doctor says to Clara after she is so awfully terrible to him?

"Go to hell."

Clara: "Fair enough. Absolutely, fair enough."

The Doctor looks at her with a quizzical look as she starts to leave: "Clara? You asked me what we're going to do. I told you. We're going to hell. Or wherever it is people go when they die…. Almost every culture in the universe has some concept of an afterlife. I always meant to have a look around, see if I could find one."

Clara (crying): "You're going to help me?"

Doctor: "Well, why wouldn't I help you?"

Clara: "Because of what I just did I just…"

Doctor (interrupting her): "You betrayed me. You betrayed my trust, you betrayed our friendship, and you betrayed everything that I've ever stood for. You let me down!"

Clara: "Then why are you helping me?"

Doctor: "Why? Do you think I care for you so little that betraying me would make a difference?"

Even after her betrayal, he still cared about her and he still tried to help her. This led to finding Missy and a weird corporation and even some Cybermen who were going to take over the universe, but he did help her. He saw this as the darkest moment, the moment when they could see what they are made of.

For all of you that have tried to demand something of God, for all of you who have sinned, and yes, that includes me, and every writer who is part of this book: do you really think that God cares for you so little that betraying Him would make a difference? Do you think God would just give up on you? Because He hasn't! Hebrews 4:16 tells us to approach the Throne of Grace with confidence. Imagine that! This God who is the all-powerful Creator of the universe and who holds the throne of eternity doesn't hold a throne of backslapping. He doesn't hold a throne of revenge. He holds a throne of grace. We cannot demand anything of Him, but we can request. We can petition. We can plead for mercy.

God's Throne is far more powerful and merciful than even the TARDIS. Go to Him in an attitude of humility, not an attitude of force.

Quest of the Day

1. Read Job 38-40.
2. If you have ever taken a prideful, forceful attitude against God, talk with Him about it. Confess this and repent of that attitude.

3. Spend some time talking with God about your needs, loved ones you miss, your dreams. Request mercy and help from Jesus.

DAY 30 – THE UNMATCHED ROBIN HOOD: WE NEED MORE THAN GOOD INTENTIONS BY CHRIS COOKE

"Suppose one of you wants to build a tower. Won't you first sit down and estimate the cost to see if you have enough money to complete it?"

Luke 14:28

According to legend, myth, and various film adaptations, Robin Hood was a noble thief. He was an incredibly virtuous man who cared for the sick and poor, who fought injustice and tyranny. We look at him as the man who stole from the rich—but it was okay because he was taking back what the rich had stolen and was returning it to the poor. Robin's intentions were good and something we could learn from. However, outside of myth, in our everyday lives, we are reminded that good intentions are not enough and can easily go awry. We see this in Scripture several times, particularly in the Book of Job with Job's friends.

So, for a quick reminder: our friend Job was a wealthy man blessed with a large family and resources, and he was "blameless and upright." As Eric mentioned in yesterday's devo, one day, Satan appeared before the Lord, who spoke of Job's goodness. Satan then argued that Job was only good because of his blessings, and that if Satan were to punish him,

Job would turn and curse the Lord. So, the Lord allowed Satan to torment Job to test this claim but forbade Satan from killing Job. Satan then, through invaders and catastrophes, kills almost everyone in Job's family except his wife, the servants, and the livestock. Job mourned but still blessed the Lord in prayers. So, Satan further tested Job through skin sores and using his wife to encourage him to "curse God and die." But Job still refused even though he was struggling.

And this is where his friends come in. See, at first, they were doing the right thing: silently supporting their mourning friend and showing love by being there. However, a despairing Job cursed the day he was born and started questioning the Lord. At this point, his friends being good support went out the window, and while their intentions were good, their actions sucked. They began accusing Job of sin and insisted that he needed to repent. When he'd rebuff their claims, they'd say he didn't understand the Lord, and they'd lecture him, which didn't encourage Job at all. It made him frustrated, more hurt, and understandably sarcastic. The friends were trying to encourage Job in the worst possible way. Their good intentions weren't enough, and their actions angered the Lord.

And that's more like most of us. The thing is, good intentions aren't ever enough. We can't just base something on "our heart being in the right place"; that's why we can't be Robin Hood. We look at Robin and we think, "Hey, I can do that! I can do X as long as Y is good." But that simply isn't the case. With Robin, we romanticize his actions, we gloss over the armed robbery aspect of what he's doing, how that would impact the guards who were just following orders, or how it briefly had further consequences upon the poor of Nottingham. We can't just trust our hearts or understand things. We need to hold our motives and actions up against the Word and our Lord to see what He says on the matter. Before meeting Christ on the road to Damascus, Paul (then Saul) was convinced that his actions —persecuting, locking up, chasing away, and voting to put the saints to death—were pure and that his intentions were good (Acts 16). But in reality, he was doing horrible things. In Acts 12, we learn that Herod put James to death. He saw that this pleased the Jews, so he imprisoned and planned to do the same to Peter. His intentions here were in theory good: he wanted to please the people. But the action to please the people would be outright sin (or as Jake Peralta on *Brooklyn Nine-Nine* so eloquently puts it, "Cool motive, still murder"). We can't sin and say, "It's okay, we're doing it for a good thing." Cool motive, still sinning.

As Christians, we have to accomplish our good intentions through God's righteous means and not our own sinful ones. We can totally take inspiration from Robin Hood and try to be like him. By many accounts, the real Robin was a very virtuous man who truly and deeply cared about the poor and the downtrodden and battled the unjust. Those are great and biblical things for us to do! However, we also can't do it the way the legends said he did. We're not a cartoon fox or Errol Flynn: our hearts can be prone to evil, and we can't gloss over or ignore the sinful, traumatizing, and hurtful aspects of our actions simply because "we meant well." We should learn from and look at Robin's virtues and his legal actions (banding together, holding leaders accountable, calling out injustice, etc.), and prayerfully take it to the Lord to learn how we can use them for His righteousness and glory.

Quest of the Day

1. Challenge and question yourself and your plans. Look honestly and deeply at what's motivating your plans.

2. Ask a close friend or mentor for their insights, take it to the Lord, and ask Him to reveal His heart and will on the matter.

3. Further, look at these Scriptures and ask yourself how you reflect them, how you practice them, and how you can live them out even better: Proverbs 16:2, Matthew 7:12, Colossians 3:17.

DAY 31 - PROTOMAN: A MELODY FROM THE PAST
BY NATHAN MARCHAND

When he told his father as well as his brothers, his father rebuked him and said, 'What is this dream you had? Will your mother and I and your brothers actually come and bow down to the ground before you?' His brothers were jealous of him, but his father kept the matter in mind.

Genesis 37:10-11

In the reimagining of the *Mega Man 3* story by The Megas (a tribute/cover band) in their album, *History Repeating: Red*, he was the first. The Protoman. The brilliant Dr. Light built him with his own hands and named him Blues. This super-robot saw the old scientist as his father. But he was not the favored son. Dr. Light later built Rock and Roll (Capcom loves punny names, can you tell?) because he saw Blues as a failed experiment. While monologuing about his brother, Protoman sings,

> They lost me
>
> Forgot me
>
> Made you from parts of me
>
> If you're The One
>
> My father's son
>
> Then what am I supposed to be?

146

(-"I'm Not the Breakman" by The Megas)

He concludes that he is a robot who simply obeys programming. His brother, now called Mega Man, seeks to become human and defends humanity from Dr. Wily and his Robot Masters. Protoman hates his brother, saying, "Killing your own won't make you human" ("I'm Not the Breakman" by The Megas).

As his brother battles the Robot Masters (all the while wrestling with his own doubts about the morality of his actions), Protoman appears and fights him to test his mettle. His rage toward Mega Man and his father seethes, reaching a boiling point when Mega Man is about to confront Dr. Wily's ultimate machine, Gamma. Protoman tells his brother, "You fight for a dream that can never be / Your arguments are noise / It's time to make your choice" ("Make Your Choice" by The Megas). And Mega Man does. He chooses not to kill Dr. Wily and to forgive their father for his mistakes, but he also tells his brother,

> Stop pretending you don't have a choice
>
> Only that can set you free
>
> And now you want to burn the world
>
> Into the ground
>
> This rage is not your destiny
>
> It's holding you down
>
> (-"I Refuse to Believe" by The Megas)

With that he goes to confront Gamma and end the war between man and machine.

The battle is fierce, but in the end Mega Man emerges triumphant. Protoman watches as his brother returns home, and he contemplates everything that's happened. It's then he has an epiphany:

> What was filled with rage finally understands
> Man is not without mistake
> Unlike that which he builds from his hands
> Though my fate is broken my path I cannot see
> Though you are the chosen
> I'll make my own history…
>
> (-"Melody from the Past" by The Megas)

He, too, forgives Dr. Light and sets his sights on forging a new destiny for himself.

This concept album has many parallels with the story of Joseph and his brothers. In Genesis 37, after boasting about a dream that showed him he, the youngest, would one day rule over his entire family, his 12 brothers conspired to kill him. One of the brothers, Reuben, instead convinced them to sell him into slavery and tell their father, Jacob, who had long favored Joseph, that he was killed by a wild animal. This would become the first in a series of events that, despite hardships and pitfalls, would lead Joseph to rise to power, becoming second only to Pharaoh in Egypt in Genesis 41. Then in one of the greatest ironies of the Bible, Joseph's brothers go to Egypt to find food, which Joseph had wisely stockpiled thanks to his dreams, during a famine (ch. 42). After a series of tests, Joseph revealed himself to them in Genesis 45. They repented of the evils they committed against him.

What about you? Are you Protoman and resentful toward any friends or family? Repent. He is quick to forgive. Or are you the one waiting for someone to reconcile with you? Pray that Jesus will lead them to repentance, because once they get right with Him, they can get right with you.

All you have to listen for the "melody from the past."

Quest of the Day

1. Read Genesis 37, 42, 45, and 50.

2. Listen to the Megas' albums *History Repeating: Blue* and *History Repeating: Red*. They can be streamed on YouTube or Spotify, among other platforms.

3. Where does there need to be reconciliation in your life, whether it's you with someone else or vice versa? Journal about this.

4. Once you've done this, take action. Pray for help and/or repentance. Then contact the other person. Be direct. Try to make a phone call or meet in person to discuss the matter.

DAY 32 - BUFFY'S ABNORMAL (BUT UNMATCHED) LIFE
BY ERIC ANDERSON

Do not grow weary in doing good, for in the proper time we will reap a harvest if we do not give up.

Galatians 6:9

All Buffy Summers wants is a normal life as a teenager, but that isn't in the cards. She has spent three years at Sunnydale High after transferring in from a school that had a fire in it (which might have started from events she was part of). Buffy is the Slayer, the one chosen to fight vampires and demons. Instead of worrying about classes, finding the right dress for this and that, or normal teenage things, she spent these years wandering in cemeteries, hunting monsters. This town was built at a "hell mouth." In fact, the school was built on it. This means the barrier between the demon dimension and Earth was weak. So, she kept fighting soulless vamps and other creatures. Over the three years at this high school, she has been captured, killed (didn't last long), hunted, challenged by other Slayers, and did I mention that she practically lives at cemeteries?

She found a boy to love…a 200-year-old vampire "boy" who had his soul given back to him so he would feel the pain of his actions as a vampire. Normal? Uh, not quite. And when he did achieve "true happiness," he turned evil again. Then he tried to destroy the world so she had to kill him to stop his scheme from sucking the world into the demon dimension. I don't imagine killing your boyfriend for going evil is normal.

In "The Prom" (season 3, episode 20), she must spend her prom night killing demon dogs so the kids at the party she wants to enjoy don't get killed. She goes out to fight but sends her friends to enjoy the prom. After fighting and killing these demon dogs, she finally gets to the party. Then something happens she would not have ever believed. The senior awards are being given out. You know, the "Class Clown" and all that. But then they announce a new award never before given to anyone. They had received notes from dozens of students. They tell her, "Buffy, we see what you have done. We know this isn't a normal high school with all sorts of weird things going on. We also know that you have always been in the middle of the weirdness, and because of your efforts, our class is blessed with the lowest mortality rate ever at Sunnydale High School. Thank you for protecting us." There is a gift, too: a decorated umbrella for the girl who had protected them from the weirdest storms of life.

Most of us don't have the life we want. Maybe you have a disease that keeps you from activities. Maybe you have a family to take care of and can't afford certain adventures.

Maybe you have kids with mental conditions that interrupt life daily. Maybe you are single in your late 30s after a lot of rejection. (Okay, that one might be me). My guess is that almost every person reading this has some area of life where they just feel like they are not normal or not happy. Perhaps you ignore it and make sure to tell everyone you are "just fine." Perhaps when you try to express your frustration people respond well, but maybe they don't. Maybe they don't understand what you are going through.

There are reluctant heroes in Scripture. As Scott discussed on day 21, Gideon was not fond of going into battle and just wanted to be left alone. God called him through "the angel of the Lord," and Gideon kept asking God to do parlor tricks to prove He was really giving him this mission. Jonah got on a boat and fled from God and found himself being toted around in the belly of a giant fish before agreeing to prophesy for God. Both of them saw success in the end, and Jonah saw it even when he didn't want it.

Jesus had tough times. He often described his disciples as "you of little faith." Can you imagine being followed around by people who are always second-guessing you? The night He was betrayed, He sat in a garden praying and told the Father "Please take this cup from me!" Essentially, "I don't want to suffer this death." But still, He also prayed, "Not my will, Father, but yours be done." He was betrayed by one of His disciples. Not just betrayed as in taking his food at dinner time, but Judas handed him over to men who wanted him dead. He put His own desires on hold to fight the terrible battle against sin and death. He even died in the battle…but then He resurrected and won the battle for eternity.

Life isn't always fun, and for some of us it rarely is enjoyable. There are a few things we can do in the middle of our frustration:

- To quote Commander Taggert in *Galaxy Quest*, "Never give up, never surrender!" Remember that we have greater things coming with Christ. "Do not grow weary in doing good" (Gal. 6:9).

- Pray, pray, pray! Jesus told God about his trepidation in the Garden of Gethsemane. David constantly complained in the Psalms. Do not be afraid to talk to God about what you want and what you need. He is a great listener, and He often surprises us in various ways.

- Talk to someone. Ignoring that something is wrong will not help. Find a confidant and share your pain and frustration with them. You might be a broken record for a time, but they might have insight for you and can at least pray for you.

More than likely someone will see what you are going through. Buffy was not just seen by her peers; when things got really bad, they joined her in the fight. Two episodes after she got that award, Sunnydale's demonic Mayor showed up at graduation, only to find the whole senior class armed and ready for battle. They were organized, armed, and ready for action.

God tends to bring help out of the woodwork for us right when we least expect it. A few years ago, I had my hardest day as a substitute teacher. It was the last day in a four-day assignment with freshman history, and each class was hard. In one class it took us 40 minutes to go through 15 minutes of notes because many kids were constantly interrupting. I kicked one or two out and others would do the same thing. During lunch I walked into the teachers' lounge, fell into a seat, and started crying. The teachers surrounded me. One teacher made sure I had a DVD to show in one class and another teacher took over a class for me while I talked with the principal and tried to process the emotions. The next week at the same building, the students and staff had the chance to participate in "The Chalkboard Project." You had a photo taken with a small chalkboard featuring a word that was hard for you (something you felt or were called by someone). During my planning hour, God told me to do it. I was reluctant. God said, "They are getting vulnerable, you should, too." I took the time to do it, and used the word "lonely." Over the next few days after this, I received private messages from students, mostly upperclassmen. The word about the bad day got out, and the

154

older kids were angry about it. Some seniors made me a card; one baked me cookies; and several students made public Facebook posts supporting me. Somehow I became the most requested sub at that school, and it is now my where I get most of my jobs. The photos from the Chalkboard Project were eventually posted in the hallways, and one day the students got to walk around to each of them. Paper covered the hard words and they wrote encouragements on it. Mine was so full, you couldn't possibly fit any more on it.

God tends to show up in unexpected ways, just like Buffy received unexpected support. Keep on swimming, look to Him, and He will take care of you.

<u>Quest of the Day</u>

1. Read Galatians 6:9 and pray it over yourself.
2. Go   to https://www.iamsecond.com/topic/contentment/ and watch a couple of the videos.
3. Think of someone you know who is not content. Find a way to encourage or help them.

DAY 33 – THOR VS. SHAZAM: BATTLES ARE BEST FOUGHT ON YOUR KNEES! BY SCOTT BAYLES

Jesus fell to the ground and prayed.

Matthew 26:39 NCV

Who would win in a fight: Superman or Hulk? Batman or Captain America? Wonder Woman or Storm? The Flash or Quicksilver? In 1996, DC and Marvel Comics teamed up to answer these and other similar questions in an epic crossover event. When a young man stumbles upon a cosmic anomaly, the DC and Marvel Universes begin to merge with some most unexpected results. With all of reality hanging in the balance, the heroes of each universe must battle each other for the fate of their own existence.

Amid many other matchups, Marvel's Thor, the mighty Asgardian "God of Thunder," is pitted against DC's Captain Marvel, the emissary of the wizard Shazam and embodiment of Olympian power. Thor and Captain Marvel stand poised—prepared to protect their respective universes. Their eyes meet. And words are exchanged.

"So," Thor announces.

"So," Captain Marvel responds.

"We understand the stakes for which we fight," Thor says. "I would wish it otherwise."

"Me too," Captain Marvel replies. "If I might ask...who are you?"

Thor answers proudly, "Thor. Son of Odin. God of Thunder. And you?"

"Captain Marvel, with the strength of Hercules, the power of Zeus, the speed of Mercury..."

"I see," Thor says. "Well, Captain.... At a moment like this...there is only one appropriate thing for those possessing the power of gods to do."

The rival champions exchange intense knowing glances, then they do it. They pray. Before any fists fly, both combatants fall to their knees, fold their hands, bow their heads and silently pray. Nestled between mighty melees and swashbuckling skirmishes, two of DC and Marvel's mightiest heroes paused and prayed.

I first read this story at the age of fifteen, and it has stuck with me ever since. As both a follower of Christ and a fan of comics, this moment spoke to me. The actions of these comic book heroes echo those of the one true superhero— Jesus.

On the night before His crucifixion, Jesus prepared Himself for what would be His greatest challenge. In a few short hours, soldiers would lead Him to a place called Golgotha, where He would be crucified. He knew exactly what was coming. Betrayal. Shame. Torture. Trauma. Loneliness.

And eventually…death. How could He face such a future without flinching? The answer—He prayed. The Bible describes it this way:

> Jesus went out as usual to the Mount of Olives, and his disciples followed him. On reaching the place… He withdrew about a stone's throw beyond them, knelt down and prayed, 'Father, if you are willing, take this cup from me; yet not my will, but yours be done.' An angel from heaven appeared to him and strengthened him. And being in anguish, he prayed more earnestly, and his sweat was like drops of blood falling to the ground (Luke 22:39-45).

Much like Thor and Captain Marvel, Jesus possesses the power of God. And, like those fictional heroes, the outcome of His upcoming battle would determine the fate of millions. So, like Thor and Captain Marvel, before beginning his bloody battle upon the cross, Jesus paused and prayed.

As Eric mentioned on days 24 and 32, his posture in Gethsemane reveals Jesus's total dependence upon God. First, He kneels down to pray. Then He falls on His face full of humility and reverence toward God. Jesus prayed so intensely that "his sweat was like drops of blood falling to the ground." As the old hymn says, "He shed no tears for His own grief, but sweat drops of blood for mine."[1] Jesus also prayed very persistently. Three times He sought God, pleading with His Father to "take this cup from me." He knew the plan. He understood what He was supposed to do, but He also acknowledged that "with God all things are possible" (Matthew 19:26). God could have changed the plan. But He didn't. This was the way it had to be. So, Jesus submitted Himself to God the Father and prayed submissively, "Not my will, but Thine, be done." In response to Christ's passionate prayers, God sent an angel to comfort and strengthen Jesus. Finally, with renewed conviction and confidence, Jesus rose from the ground and stood tall—ready to conquer the cross.

We could certainly learn from these examples. We each have our own personal challenges and conflicts awaiting us. Before the battle begins, each of us ought to pause and pray. The Bible says, "Don't worry about anything; instead, pray about everything. Tell God what you need, and thank him for all he has done. Then you will experience God's peace, which exceeds anything we can understand" (Philippians 4:6 NLT). Prayer may not remove our challenges, but it will give us the power and peace to face them head on.

Quest of the Day

1. Read Matthew 26:36-46.

---

[1] *I Stand Amazed in the Presence* by Chas. H. Gabriel (1905)

2. Why does Jesus pray the same prayer three times? Why is it significant that Jesus prayed "not my will, but your will be done"? Have you ever prayed with the kind of passion and intensity that Jesus prayed with?

3. What battles are you facing? Spend some time today in prayer. Share your conflicts and concerns with God, then face your future with confidence.

DAY 34 - ARAGORN: THE KING OF THE DEAD BY DARRIN BALL

The last enemy to be destroyed is death.

I Corinthians 15:26

If you visited a church and someone there asked you, "What brings you here?" what would their reaction be if you proclaimed, "I am here to worship the LORD of the Dead!"? Maybe you showed up wearing medieval armor as well to add to the effect.

The Paths of the Dead from the chapter "The Passing of the Grey Company" in *The Return of the King* is one of the most intriguing sections in *The Lord of the Rings*. Aragorn openly proclaims his title before the doors of Edoras. He gazes into the Palantir, the Stone of Orthanc, and beholds Sauron himself. Sauron would strike more quickly now, knowing that the heir of Isildur lives and wields the sword of Elendil. Aragorn is reminded of the Paths of the Dead. There is no time to follow with Théoden. Aragorn learns many things wrestling with the Dark Lord Sauron, and he knows of an unseen peril coming from the south upon Minas Tirith. Elrond sends word through his sons to Aragorn to "remember the words of the seer and the Paths of the Dead."

Éowyn could not understand. "But this is madness," she says. From her point of view, the living could not pass

161

through the Paths of the Dead. Before arriving at Dunharrow, Aragorn explains to Gimli and Legolas, "The living have never used that road since the coming of the Rohirrim...for it is closed to them. But in this dark hour the heir of Isildur may use it, if he dare." He does not take it gladly, but need is driving him.

Over 3,000 years earlier, the Men of the Mountains had been under an oath to fight with Isildur against the Dark Lord Sauron. They broke their oath because they had worshiped Sauron in the Dark Years. Isildur put them under a curse never to rest until their oath was fulfilled. He placed the stone of Erech there as a symbol bringing the terror of the Sleepless Dead to those dwelling around the Hill of Erech. They knew a curse lay on the Paths of the Dead.

By the mighty will of Aragorn, the Grey Company passes into the realm of the dead. Nothing attacks them, but if they ever halted, there seemed an endless whisper of voices all around them. After kneeling before the bones of what had been a mighty man, Aragorn rebukes the whispers and summons them to the Stone of Erech to fulfill their vow. When they emerge from the Paths of the Dead, they are not alone. Legolas notes, "The Dead are following...I see shapes of Men and of horses, and pale banners like shreds of cloud, and spears like winter-thickets on a misty night. The Dead are following."

There is a terror over the land as the Dead follow Aragorn. People cry out, "The King of the Dead! The King of the Dead is come upon us!" Aragorn is undaunted by the Dead. "Oathbreakers, why have you come?" The answer is, "To fulfill our oath and have peace." Aragorn commands them to follow him into battle so their oath will be fulfilled. The black standard is unveiled, and Aragorn leads the Dead through Gondor into the day that brought no dawn. The people in that region flee at the rumor of the coming of the King of the Dead.

Sometimes the movie has to be different than the book, and that's okay. The movie took a bit of creative license, but the original intent was preserved. In both cases, Aragorn, as the rightful king, descends into the realm of the Dead. Instead of the Dead preventing him from emerging, the Dead arise and follow him. He becomes the King of the Dead by taking the Paths of the Dead. In the movie, there was one representative of the Dead who materializes and speaks to Aragorn. This is fitting because in the book one voice answered and spoke for all.

Where did Tolkien get his idea? Ancient paganism? From the Greek and Roman pantheons, which had a god of the underworld? How about right out of the pages of the Bible?

In Scripture, death is not just a state of being, but a place. Job 38:17, Psalm 9:13 and 107:18, and Isaiah 38:10

contain the phrase "the gates of death." In Psalm 88, death is compared to a giant pit where the dead can walk around, yet they have no strength to ascend. In other words, it's a one-way trip; you go down, but you don't come back up. However, Psalm 33:2-3 shows that God has the ability to heal and bring someone up from this pit. Ezekiel 32:17-32 contains a vivid description of this place, also termed the lower (nether) parts of the Earth. Instead of the multitude of Egypt being killed and passing out of existence, Ezekiel sees a vision of them in the realm of the dead. Ezekiel could look down and see the dead. They were gone from the land of the living in the depths of the Earth alongside all the other wicked dead, just like the Oathbreakers, the Sleepless Dead dwelling in the mountain.

After the death of Christ on the cross, Jesus descended into the realm of the dead (Ephesians 4:8-10). Instead of the dead impeding Him, the dead arose and followed Him as He ascended. While there, He preached to the spirits who were imprisoned (I Peter 4:18-20). When the Apostle John was old, the Glorified Christ appeared to him and said, "I am the Living One; I was dead, and now look, I am alive for ever and ever! And I hold the keys of death and Hades" (Revelation 1:18).

Romans 14:8-9 teaches us the supremacy of Christ over all things, both living and dead. The verses read, "If we live, we live for the Lord; and if we die, we die for the Lord. So, whether we live or die, we belong to the Lord. For this very reason, Christ died and returned to life so that he might be the Lord of both the dead and the living." You see that? Jesus Christ died in order to be sovereign over death. This was a demonstration that there is no realm, not even the realm of death, that is unconquerable by Him. One of the titles of Jesus Christ is "The LORD of the Dead."

When you think of death, are you like Gimli? He confesses, "My blood runs chill." The horses were terrified as well, and only out of love for their riders did they submit. Yet Gimli had hope as long as he kept his eyes on Aragorn. "Does he feel no fear?" Gimli asks.

Does death terrify you? You may be thinking of the death of a loved one, a family member, or your own death. Is there someone whose death would devastate you, perhaps shatter your faith? Understand that death is a place that Jesus Christ has visited and conquered. This is not mythology or a story; it is the truth. *For the Christian, to die is to pass from one realm of Christ's authority into another. He is LORD of the Living and the LORD of the Dead.*

Quest of the Day

1. Read Psalm 90:12 and James 4:13-15 and contemplate your mortality. Talk to God about your physical death. Talk with a close friend about your death. Journal about the legacy you would like to leave.

2. Read 1 Corinthians 15:51-58 and contemplate the immortality of those who belong to Jesus Christ. Talk to God about eternal life. Talk with a close friend about living forever. Journal about how God is equipping you to serve Him for all eternity.

DAY 35 – RAND AL'THOR: THE BURDEN OF SALVATION
BY NICK HAYDEN

"Come to me, all who labor and are heavy laden, and I will give you rest. Take my yoke upon you, and learn from me, for I am gentle and lowly in heart, and you will find rest for your souls. For my yoke is easy, and my burden is light."

Matthew 11:28-30 (ESV)

In the epic fantasy series *The Wheel of Time* (which everyone should read), Rand al'Thor is the prophesied Dragon Reborn, a savior destined to save the world from the Dark One—and also destined to break all the old bindings between peoples and nations throughout the world while doing so. Also, bonus: the magic he uses will eventually drive him mad.

But Rand is originally just a farm kid from the middle of nowhere. (Isn't that how these things always go?) As he realizes his fate and begins to take on the burden of becoming the one who will sever all the old ties so that the world might survive the Last Battle, he adopts a traditional warrior saying: "Duty is heavier than a mountain, death lighter than a feather." The weight of being a savior, of knowing that the fate of nations rests on you, is immeasurably heavy. He, and he alone, stands against the victory of the Dark One.

The outcome of history doesn't normally depend on us, but many times we bear a similar burden—the weight of being our own savior, of deciding our own fate. As Christians, we can become paralyzed by questions like, "Do I read the Bible enough?" "Do I pray enough?" "Have I told enough people about Jesus?" "Have I avoided lustful thoughts?" "Am I in God's will?" "Am I good enough?"

Depending on your own bent toward guilt or perfectionism and your local church culture, these questions can multiply and swarm until you feel unable to bear the weight. But you must soldier on. That's what good Christians do. Sure, Jesus forgave me, but see what a mess I've made of it! I'll keep trying, trying, trying. I force a smile and keep striving. Why am I such an unworthy, miserable sinner?

It is to you, miserable sinner, unworthy farm boy from the middle of somewhere, that Jesus comes to and says, "Come to me..., and I will give you rest." He has already borne the weight of the world. He has already been raised in obscurity and taken on the mantle of prophecy and fate. He has already been broken for the salvation of the world and destroyed the dividing wall between people. He has conquered the Dark One.

Is this the same old Gospel truth? Of course it is. Do we need to hear it again? I do. All the time. Because it is so very easy to try to be your own savior, to assume everything depends on you, that you are the hero of your own story. But Jesus is the hero of our story.

The Christian life is surely about taking up your cross, about putting on the armor of faith, but it is also about resting in the One who already did the work, "for whoever has entered God's rest has also rested from his works as God did from his. Let us therefore strive to enter that rest… " (Hebrews 4:10-11).

Rest. The Chosen One has already done the work. Trust in Him.

Quest of the Day

1. Examine yourself. In what areas of life are you striving without God? Give them to Jesus.

2. Find a time to take a Sabbath rest, whether for a day a week, an hour a day, or ten minutes before you rush into the day's activities. Set the time purposely aside.

3. Take a piece of paper and draw a line down the center. On one half, write your burdens. One the other side, write a promise of God for each burden. Ask a pastor or friend to help find promises that apply if you don't know of one.

DAY 36 – THE UNMATCHED ARTHUR: THE ONE TRUE KING!
BY SCOTT BAYLES

On his robe and on his thigh he has this name written: King of kings and Lord of lords.

Revelation 19:16

The innovative new tabletop game Unmatched: Battle of Legends pits unlikely opponents against each other in deck-building combat. The first volume includes iconic characters like Alice (of *Alice in Wonderland* fame), Sinbad, Medusa, and King Arthur. (You might have noticed that these and other characters featured in the game have been the subjects of some of the devotions in this book). Of these legendary figures, I find King Arthur the most intriguing and inspirational.

According to legend, there once lived a benevolent king named Uther-Pendragon. He assembled many valiant knights, conquered all his foes, and ruled all of England with justice and mercy. King Uther-Pendragon sired two daughters and a son. But before the birth of his son, the King received a visit from the great wizard and wise man, Merlin. Merlin counseled the king, saying, "This must be a secret birth." His face clouded with worry, Merlin explained that the King would soon fall sick and die. The child would be defenseless and likely killed by one of Uther-Pendragon's enemies. So, when the

170

child was born, the king secretly entrusted him to Merlin's care. In a few short months, Merlin's prophecy came to pass. The noble King faced his death with courage and grace.

In the years that followed, the realm fell into chaos. With no apparent heir to the throne, lesser kings contended to become overlord. Wicked knights and barons terrorized the peasants and travelers. Knights fought one another in bloody battles, not for honor but for personal profit. Injustice ruled. People longed for a new and just king to rule the land, which groaned with the terrible trouble that lay upon it.

When it seemed as if the land could no longer bear the strain, the Archbishop called upon Merlin to use his mighty wisdom to heal the land and help find a king. "My lord Archbishop," Merlin answered, "the spirit of prophecy moves me now to say that this country shall soon have a king who will be even wiser and greater and more worthy of praise than Uther-Pendragon. This ruler shall bring order and peace where there is now disorder and war, and he shall be of Uther-Pendragon's own royal blood." Merlin continued, "I will use my magic to create an obstacle, which, if any man shall solve it, the world will know that man as the rightful king and overlord of this realm."

Then, in a swirl of magic, Merlin conjured a huge marble slab with an iron stone upon it. Thrust into the stone was a wondrous sword with a hilt that flashed in the sunlight.

Chiseled into the marble slab was an inscription: "Whosoever pulleth out this sword from the stone that same is rightwise king-born of England."

On Christmas morning, thousands gathered as dozens of kings and dukes from across the land attempted to lift the sword from the stone on display in the cathedral. One by one, they grasped the hilt and tugged with all their might, but the sword remained firmly fixed within the stone. Some were infuriated by their failure; others embarrassed.

Finally, Merlin entered the cathedral, followed by a teenage boy in flame-colored robes. "Arise, Arthur," Merlin called out. At that, young Arthur stepped forward, wrapped his fingers around the hilt of the sword and, in one quick movement, drew the sword out of the stone with grace and ease, and swung it about his head. The crowd cheered and clapped with such force that the earth itself seemed to tremble. The kings and dukes displayed mixed reactions. Most willingly acknowledged Arthur as the true king, while others felt jealous and indignant. Despite their complaints, though, the Archbishop proclaimed Arthur the true and rightful King of England.

King Arthur went on to become the most benevolent and beloved king in all the realms, leading his twelve knights of justice on grand adventures and daring conquests. But what

I find most compelling is that King Arthur bears some striking similarities to the One True King—Jesus Christ.

The Bible proclaims that Jesus is "the ruler of the kings of the earth" (Revelation 1:5), and, "he is Lord of lords and King of kings" (Revelation 17:14). Like Arthur, Jesus is King by royal blood and had to be whisked away as an infant to protect Him from those who wanted Him dead. Just as Merlin prophesied the coming of King Arthur, the Old Testament prophets predicted the coming of King Jesus hundreds of years before His birth. And, like Arthur, King Jesus is "even wiser and greater and more worthy of praise" than any lesser king.

The only problem is, if Jesus is King, that means I'm not. Like those disappointed dukes, we don't always like that. We all want to be the king to some extent. Some of us want to be the king of our workplace, or the king of our house. Some of us want to be the king of our tabletop gaming group. Some of us treat the highway as our own little kingdom, demanding that peasants ask our permission before they change lanes or slow down. But the truth is, whether we choose to accept it or not, there is only One True King. It's not me. It's not you. Jesus alone reigns as King of kings and Lord of lords.

That's a good thing because none of us are fit to wield the sword or wear the crown. Jesus, and Jesus alone, is worthy to rule. He's loving, merciful, just, and true. And the best part is—He invites all of us into his Kingdom.

Quest of the Day

1. Read John 12:12-19 and John 18:37.

2. What other similarities do you see between King Arthur and King Jesus? Differences?

3. If Jesus is truly King of all creation, including your life and mine, how should we respond to Him?

4. If you haven't surrendered yourself to Christ's Lordship, consider doing so today. If you've already accepted Christ as Lord, examine your life to be sure you're living by Kingdom values and principles.

DAY 37 - CALLING ON THE LORD LIKE THE BAT-FAM CALLS ON ORACLE
BY CHRIS COOKE

And call on me in the day of trouble; I will deliver you, and

you will honor me.

Psalm 50:15 NIV

Unless you're a fan of the Bat-Family or the excellent Rocksteady *Arkham Series* of video games, you might be wondering, "Who is Oracle?" I'm going to give a bit of her backstory, as she has more famous aliases and identities. Oracle is the (twice now) former best-known Batgirl, Barbara Gordon. In the excellent, controversial, and originally out-of-continuity one-shot story *The Killing Joke* by Alan Moore, Babs is paralyzed and then tortured by the Joker. This development is one of the most hard-hitting aspects of the story. It also marked a very painful year for Batman, as just nine months later the Joker killed Jason Todd, the second Robin, in another well-known story, *A Death in The Family* by Jim Starlin. Unlike Jason Todd, though, who 51% of fans had voted to be killed off, people loved Barbara and were very upset about what happened to her. For some, such as writer Gail Simone, it sparked and contributed to the needed conversation about the treatment female comic characters receive in comparison to male characters. For others, such as comic editor/writer wife and husband duo of Kim Yale and John Ostrander, their distaste for how Babs was treated inspired them to make sure that she didn't simply fade into obscurity, and over the next few years after *The Killing Joke*, her Oracle persona was born.

Now operating as an information broker for many law enforcement agencies and superheroes, Barbara's genius-level intellect, photographic memory, and expert hacking and decrypting skills are put to a very different use than when she was Batgirl. She is now at a level where she is seen as Batman's equal intellectually; has a hand in training the new Batgirl, the fan favorite character Casandra Cain; forming the Birds of Prey; and assisting many characters across the DC landscape (looking at you, Martian Manhunter). Then a retcon in the controversial New 52 company-wide shakeup (because comics) allowed her to walk again after three years of intense physical therapy and reclaim the mantle of Batgril in 2011, a role she still fills as of this writing. Barbara has recently, starting in *Batman* #100, in the fallout of the *Joker War* (by James Tynion IV), reclaimed her Oracle identity as well, operating as both while she figures out where she is best used.

As I mentioned, Orcale was also used heavily in the three Rocksteady *Arkham* video games. She operated much like she did in the comics, as Batman's additional eyes and ears, and she was needed to get things done. At points you, the player, simply couldn't progress, level up, or access certain items or areas without her assistance. You were *constantly* calling on her for aid, getting her input, and acting under her advice. In DLC levels for *Arkham City* and *Arkham Knight*, where you operated as Robin (Tim Drake) or Nightwing (Dick Grayson), you bet they were deferring to her help. And in *Arkham Knight*, when certain twists happen involving her, you bet people were both heart punched *and* later relieved.

Oracle is an invaluable asset to her team, but with all due respect to her, we as believers have a direct line to a much greater (and, you know, non-fictional) and more incredible source of not only information and support but also love, wisdom, forgiveness, sharpening, grace, forgiveness, salvation, and so much more.

Scripture reminds us time and time again to call upon the Lord, in numerous different ways and contexts, whether it be provision, repentance, salvation, strength, seeking, and so, *so*, many more. Here are some wonderful reminders from the Word:

- "The Lord is near to all who call on him to all who call on him in truth" (Psalm 145:18 ESV).
- "Before they call I will answer; while they are yet speaking I will hear" (Isaiah 65:24).
- "You, Lord, are forgiving and good, abounding in love to all who call to you" (Psalm 86:5).

My final encouragement is this: as much I love Batman (and the Bat-Fam), I gotta say, while not necessarily cocky, Batman is stubborn, obsessive, and not necessarily humble. He knows how smart he is because of how often he is right and can have a very "my way or the highway" view of things. And yet he *still* calls on Oracle. If a dude like that can open himself up to help, how much more ready and willing should we make ourselves to do so with the Lord?

More. Much, much more.

Quest of the Day

1. Look at and ask friends what areas in your life you need to call for assistance in.

2. Pray for clarity on these issues.

3. Write them down, memorize them, pray through them, and in whatever way works best for you actually call on one of your resources.

4. In a week or a month, check in with those trusted loved ones and see how you're doing from their perspective.

DAY 38 - NO GELFLING IS AN ISLAND
BY NICK HAYDEN

Rejoice with those who rejoice, weep with those who weep.

Romans 12:15

The '80s gave us many wonderful things, including a variety of trippy and experimental fantasy movies. One of these creations, *The Dark Crystal*, from the brain of Muppet-creator Jim Henson, showed us the beautiful and exotic world of Thra, but it was not until Netflix's prequel *Dark Crystal: Age of Resistance* that audiences experienced the full range of creatures that populated that world.

One of these races is the Gelflings. These humanoid, vaguely elfish creatures exist as seven distinct clans. As *Age of Resistance* begins, these clans are largely separated. They exist peaceably with one another, but distinctly from one another. They have developed unique cultures and largely tend to their own, looking down on other clans.

It is not until the Darkening, when the Crystal that is the heart of life on the planet begins to fail, that the Gelflings start to join together. In the war against their enemy, the Skeksis, they learn to trust in one another. This is accomplished in part through dreamfasting. When two Gelflings dreamfast, they telepathically share memories in a stream of consciousness. They intimately share their experiences with one another.

Christians are called to this same intimate understanding and support of one another. Paul encouraged the Roman Christians to "[r]ejoice with those who rejoice, weep with those who weep" (Romans 12:15). We are to share our joys and sorrows with one another, not just intellectually, but emotionally and truly.

Yet this is not easy for individualistic, selfish humans. When someone is sad, we don't want to be sad with them. Many times, we would rather help them "get over it." And when someone is happy, our first reaction is not always to share their joy. Sometimes, it's to be jealous of their blessing, whether it's a new job or a new relationship or a new "toy." It is much easier to stay in our own little world, just as the Gelflings stayed in their own homogenous clans, than to come alongside someone who is in a different place than we are emotionally.

Jesus shows us otherwise. He willingly "emptied himself, by taking the form of a servant, being born in the likeness of men" (Philippians 2:7). He experienced birth and childhood and teenage years; He worked and walked; He drank wine at weddings and wept at the tomb of a good friend; He suffered and died. He knows our temptations, our joys and fears and sorrows—not just intellectually, but experientially.

And He calls us to be part of a community, a brotherhood, a family called the Church, and to likewise share our lives with one another.

If you follow Jesus, it cannot be just you and Him. It is you and Him and others. We pray "Our Father" and not "My Father." Let us learn to dreamfast with one another, for the building up of each other and for God's glory.

<u>Quest of the Day</u>

1. Do you know of someone who is going through a rough time? Be proactive in contacting them. Use the most direct way possible. Prefer phone over text, one-to-one over social media.

2. Educate yourself on the Church in the larger world. Christians in many other countries are suffering trials and persecution. It's easy to focus on our own needs. In prayer, focus on the needs of those Christians you haven't met.

DAY 39 - DR. GRANT THE CALLOUSED PALEONTOLOGIST
BY BECKY SMITH

Therefore, as God's chosen people, holy and dearly loved,

clothe yourselves with compassion, kindness, humility,

gentleness and patience.

Colossians 3:12

"If you wanted to scare the kid, you could've pulled a gun on him," says Dr. Ellie Sattler.

The scene opens with our two main protagonists doing what they do best: digging up dinosaurs. Dr. Grant and Dr. Sattler, with their team of volunteers and interns, gather around a "state of the art" machine that gives them a visual of a buried Velociraptor fossil. Dr. Grant muses on the physiological structure and similarities between the extinct biped and its near-cousin, modern-day birds. A prepubescent boy pipes up in the back: "That doesn't look very scary. More like a six foot turkey." The crowd parts, leaving a clear path for Dr. Grant to slowly stalk closer as he begins to describe the hunting technique of this "six foot turkey." He circles his prey, pulling out of his pocket the curved six-inch claw for which the Velociraptor is known. He commands the boy's attention, disemboweling him, castrating him, sending the clear message that he, Dr. Grant, is the expert, and the boy is merely there to keep quiet and learn, or be devoured.

In the 1993 blockbuster hit, *Jurassic Park*, we see a portrayal of Dr. Alan Grant that is quite unlike the original source material by Michael Crichton. This Dr. Grant is a bit more crotchety, joyless, and cold, especially towards children. The many attempts by Dr. Sattler to pair him up with Lex and Tim, the two grandchildren of the park's visionary, are met with disdain. Tim, the precocious junior paleontologist, clearly idolizes Dr. Grant and tries to engage him with some of his knowledge, all the while attempting to ride in the same vehicle as Dr. Grant. Later, after they exit the vehicles, Lex even feigns to trip, and Dr. Grant's instinct kicks in and grabs her hand. He tries to let go, but she holds on tight as they trek through the brush to see the sick Triceratops. We catch a rare glimpse of Dr. Grant's childlike love for dinosaurs as he listens to the Trike's heartbeat.

As the movie progresses, we see a drastic change—and it all starts when the T-rex attacks. The bloodsucking lawyer, who was paired up with the kids in the first vehicle, abandons them and runs for his life. The T-rex demolishes the first Ford Explorer trying to get at the children while Malcolm and Dr. Grant, mesmerized, watch in horror from the second Explorer. Finally, Dr. Grant breaks the spell and decides to act. Between him and Malcolm, they are able to get the T-rex away from the kids, consequently leading her to the cowering lawyer, who ultimately meets his doom in the jaws of The Tyrant Lizard King.

Now the adventure truly begins. Dr. Grant leads the frightened children through the park, meeting, hiding, and running from the many denizens of Ingen's cloning and gene manipulation. As he does so, his tone grows softer, his hands willingly clasping those of the children, and his smile grows warmer. He is even seen throwing away the deadly claw that he used in the beginning to "educate" the smart-aleck boy at the dig site. At the culmination, he finally puts himself in between the children and the attacking Velociraptors, knowing that his end will be a gruesome one, but hoping to save the children nonetheless. We all know the end. The T-rex makes her third and final entrance and attacks the raptors, allowing the survivors to escape.

The final scene shows us the exhausted kids, their heads resting on Dr. Grant's shoulders, his arms wrapped protectively around them as he smiles knowingly at Dr. Sattler. What a change!

Paul, the author of the small book of Colossians, instructs the members of the church in Colossae, encouraging them on their journey through the Christian life. As with all Scripture, the Holy Spirit speaks to us today as well. Colossians

3:1-17 touches on many things regarding the believer's walk with God, but my focus here is on verses 12 through 17.

As we grow older and more mature, whether physically, mentally and/or spiritually, we will face many trials, reminding us constantly that we live in a fallen world and feel the effects of sin that permeates everything around us. As an older Christian, I sometimes forget what it was like to be young and naive to the dangers and trials of the world. I also often forget the excitement and boundless joy one experiences upon their first meeting with Jesus the Savior.

Not unlike the Dr. Grant we see in the beginning, us older Christians can become cold, full of ourselves and our gained experience and knowledge, and even view the younger, newer Christian with contempt. May it not be so! When that newer Christian says something in their ignorance that is false, we should not berate or humiliate them but lovingly correct and encourage them. When the young Christian comes to us for advice with questions or with just the simple desire to share in the joy in learning about Jesus, we should not avoid them or try to pass them off but guide them and protect them and relish in the childlike joy that is given to those who are redeemed.

Paul uses words like, "compassion, kindness, humility, gentleness, patience, [and] love." Does this all sound familiar? To the well-read Christian, these are all Fruit of the Spirit, which Paul talks about in Galatians. The Fruit of the Spirit are all outward expressions of the change that has been wrought in our hearts by the New Birth. This Fruit is to be on full display and cultivated along with our brothers and sisters in Christ.

The trials we face are to grow us, mature us, mold us into the image of our Lord Jesus, but also used to help other, younger Christians; to encourage, impart wisdom, guide and comfort; all with the compassion, kindness, patience, and love for one another, to which Paul calls us. So, when those T-rex-sized trials come, when the Velociraptors of sin and temptation give chase, let's grasp hands together, lift each other up, protect, guide, and teach one another with compassion and love. Be like the new Dr. Grant. Throw away the claw of contempt and remember what it was like to be overjoyed when first meeting your Savior!

Quest of the Day

1. Read Colossians 3:1-17.
2. Write on 3x5 cards the passage Colossians 3:12-17 and commit it to memory.
3. Turn to Galatians 5:22-23 and compare the Fruit of the Spirit with the above Colossians passage. Write down the similarities and pray, asking God to bear fruit in your life.

DAY 40 - THE OBLIVAEON/RAGNAROK/PAROUSIA PARALLEL BY DARRIN BALL

I am the Alpha and the Omega, the First and the Last, the
Beginning and the End.

Revelation 22:13

Greater Than Games (GTG), publisher of the popular cooperative card game Sentinels of the Multiverse (SOTM), announced that Oblivaeon would come to the Multiverse to end everything. The end that Oblivaeon brings is twofold. First, Oblivaeon is a boundless cosmic entity from far beyond the physical realms with a singular purpose: to end all of time and space. The Oblivaeon expansion would introduce a new way to play Sentinels. Assemble your heroes and try to defeat Oblivaeon before he destroys all realities, especially the "one in which the heroes of earth have banded together in defense of not just their planet, not just their galaxy, but the Multiverse itself." Second, GTG announced that this would be the end of Sentinels Comics, with no more expansions for SOTM after this. It was the end of the Multiverse in more than one way.

The result escalated to $1.5 million pledged on Kickstarter. With the unanticipated resources, GTG put out a grand finale for SOTM. Oblivaeon was not only an entity, it was an event. It was the end of everything as we knew it.

187

"Whispers of Oblivaeon" had been echoing in the head of Infinitor, which drove him crazy. Progeny took the "form of the harbinger" to let them know that the "hour of reckoning" had come to "face the inevitable" "beginning of the end." Now, Oblivaeon announces, "Cease your meddling! You cannot push back against the end of all things!" (*Freedom Five* #797).

Ragnarök is also an event. Some may have misunderstood the title of *Thor: Ragnarök* in thinking that Ragnarök was the bad guy that Thor would fight. Ragnarök comes from Norse mythology. It is the end of all that is but also the beginning of a new world. The world that emerges will be fresh and fertile with no need to sow crops as they spring forth from the earth on their own. Thor tried with all his might to prevent Ragnarök. He defeated Surtur and took his crown back to Asgard, believing Ragnarök was prevented. The event seems predestined, though, as what Thor did only ensured that Ragnarök eventually transpired.

Hans Christian Andersen frequently borrowed from Norse mythology. In *The Marsh King's Daughter*, Helga (a pagan who is transformed into a Christian) has a vision of what will occur at this time:

> All these thoughts took form in her dreams,
> and it seemed to her that she was still awake,
> sitting thoughtfully upon her bed while

darkness reigned without. A storm arose. She heard the rolling of the waves east and west of her from the North Sea and from the waters of the Cattegat. The monstrous serpent which, according to her faith, encompassed the earth in the depths of the ocean, was trembling in convulsions from the dread of Ragnarök, the night of the gods. He personified the Day of Judgment, when everything should pass away, even the great gods themselves. The war horn sounded, and away over the rainbow rode the gods, clad in steel, to fight their last battle. Before them flew the shield maidens, the Valkyries, and the ranks were closed by the phantoms of the dead warriors. The whole atmosphere shone in the radiance of the northern lights, but darkness conquered in the end.... The air resounded with the clashing of sword and club and the whistling of arrows, as though a fierce hailstorm were passing over them. The hour had come when heaven and earth were to pass away, the stars to fall, and everything to succumb to Surtur's fire. And yet a new earth and a new heaven would arise, and fields of corn would wave where the seas now rolled over the golden sands. The God whom none might name would reign, and to Him would ascend Baldur the mild, the loving, redeemed from the kingdom of the dead. He was coming!

It's a telling scene in *Thor: Ragnarök* when Thor realizes that Asgard must be destroyed in order to save his people, the true Asgard. Hela, the goddess of death, is too mighty and has become empowered by Asgard. To save his people from the power of death, the world that he loves must be destroyed through Ragnarök, being consumed by Surtur's flames.

Mythology is fun to think about, but let's consider the reality of Jesus Christ. Jesus has promised to come again. The Greek word used for the coming of Christ is *Parousia*, which not only means "coming" but also an actual, physical presence. Basically, Jesus is coming to stay this time. There are quite a few similarities between the coming of Jesus Christ and the "end of it all" that we see in both Oblivaeon and Ragnarök. Note how many times you find identical terminology between Andersen's description of Ragnarök and the following passage in 2 Peter 3:9-14:

> The Lord is not slow in keeping his promise, as some understand slowness. Instead he is patient with you, not wanting anyone to perish, but everyone to come to repentance. But the

day of the Lord will come like a thief. The heavens will disappear with a roar; the elements will be destroyed by fire, and the earth and everything done in it will be laid bare. Since everything will be destroyed in this way, what kind of people ought you to be? You ought to live holy and godly lives as you look forward to the day of God and speed its coming. That day will bring about the destruction of the heavens by fire, and the elements will melt in the heat. But in keeping with his promise we are looking forward to a new heaven and a new earth, where righteousness dwells. So then, dear friends, since you are looking forward to this, make every effort to be found spotless, blameless and at peace with him.

Just as Oblivaeon was both a person and an event, so is Jesus Christ, except obviously that Jesus isn't evil. In Revelation 1:8 (echoing Isaiah 41:4) Jesus declares, "I am Alpha and Omega, the beginning and the ending" (KJV). *Jesus is the ending. He is the period at the end of the sentence. He is the end of the age, the end of this world.*

Studying Ragnarök in Norse theology could be quite time-consuming, as some of it is described in poetry and art. Before the first coming of Jesus Christ, the end of this age was contained in the poetry of the Psalms. Consider this apocalyptic imagery:

> The Mighty One, God, the LORD,
>
> speaks and summons the earth
>
> from the rising of the sun to where it sets.
>
> From Zion, perfect in beauty,
>
> God shines forth.
>
> Our God comes and will not be silent;
>
> a fire devours before him,
>
> and around him a tempest rages.
>
> He summons the heavens above,
>
> and the earth, that he may judge his people:
>
> (Psalm 50:1-4)

> Let the heavens rejoice, let the earth be glad;
>
> let the sea resound, and all that is in it.
>
> Let the fields be jubilant, and everything in them;
>
> let all the trees of the forest sing for joy.
>
> Let all creation rejoice before the LORD, for he comes,
>
> he comes to judge the earth.
>
> He will judge the world in righteousness
>
> and the peoples in his faithfulness.
>
> (Psalm 96:11-13)

The LORD reigns, let the earth be glad;

let the distant shores rejoice.

Clouds and thick darkness surround him;

righteousness and justice are the foundation of

his throne.

Fire goes before him

and consumes his foes on every side.

His lightning lights up the world;

the earth sees and trembles.

The mountains melt like wax before the

LORD,

before the Lord of all the earth.

(Psalm 97:1-5)

In poetic form, the psalmist saw the LORD coming to put an end to this world and begin a new one. Our world looks pretty crazy right now, but those who believe and trust in the LORD Jesus Christ have this hope. *He will come. He is the ending. When we understand that this world is under the curse of death, we better understand why it must be destroyed and renewed in order to save God's people.*

Have fun and stay busy ~ Luke 19:13

-The Orange Mailman

Quest of the Day

1. Read 1 John 2:15-17 for hope beyond this world.

2. Think about whether you are living for this temporary world or for the eternal world to come. Make a list of things in your life that are aligned with this temporary world. Make another list of things that are aligned with God's kingdom.

3. Find a way to talk with someone about how Jesus Christ will come again. Consider using a parallel like Ragnarök, Oblivaeon, or some other example you see.

DAY 41 - THE MANDALORIAN: THIS IS THE WAY BY NATHAN MARCHAND

Whether you turn to the right or to the left, your ears will hear a voice behind you, saying, "This is the way; walk in it."

Isaiah 30:21

"Bounty hunting is a complicated profession," the Client says, surrounded by Imperial Stormtroopers.

That's putting it lightly.

Din Djarin, known better as "the Mandalorian" or just "Mando," is an armor-clad man wandering the galaxy on assignments for anyone who pays well. He seems to take no pleasure in his work, but nor does he hate it. It's simply a job. "I can bring you in warm, or I can bring you in cold," he tells one unfortunate target. He rarely speaks, and his past is a mystery. But what Greef Karga and the bounty hunters guild knows is he gets the job done.

That all changed when he was sent by the Client to retrieve a 50-year-old quarry. After surviving a shootout with bandits and blasting rival bounty hunter droid IG-11 in the head, the Mandalorian discovers that his target is a child—one *Star Wars* fans dubbed "Baby Yoda" even after his true name was revealed in the show's second season, as Scott mentioned on day 21. Mando does give the Child to the Client, although he's never told why the Client wants him or what he will do to the Child. The Mandalorian returns to his people's enclave, where he asks the Armorer to use the beskar metals he collected from the bounty to make him new armor and donate some to their clan's foundlings.

"As it should always be," says the Armorer. "The foundlings are the future. This is the way."

"This is the way!" repeat the other Mandalorians.

"This is the way," says Mando.

An orphan himself, Mando returns to the Client's hideout after a crisis of conscience and rescues the Child. This makes him a target for the entire bounty hunters guild. He escapes with the Child. During a series of adventures trying to learn the Child's identity, the little one saves Mando several times using strange supernatural powers. Mando understands, if only a little, why the Imperial remnants want the foundling. Eventually, they return to the Mandalorian enclave. There the armorer tells Mando he must reunite the Child with his own kind, which she says is "an order of sorcerers called Jedi."

"You expect me to search the galaxy and deliver this creature to a race of enemy sorcerers?" asks Mando.

"This is the way."

In Isaiah 30, the titular prophet pronounced God's judgment on Israel. He called them "obstinate" and said they "heap sin upon sin" (v. 1). They'd turned to idols (v. 22) and refused to listen to the Lord's instruction (v. 9). If the prophets told them anything bad, they wouldn't hear it and begged them to tell them only good things (v. 10). But in verse 18, Isaiah pivoted: "Yet the LORD longs to be gracious to you; he rises to show you compassion. For the LORD is a God of justice. Blessed are all who wait on Him!" He then listed blessings that God would bestow to them after their affliction. Amidst that is today's key verse: "Whether you turn to the right or to the left, your ears will hear a voice behind you, saying, '*This is the way*; walk in it'" (v. 21, emphasis added).

Din Djaran and his people lived a hard life. Their planet was purged during the Clone Wars. The Mandalorians were scattered across the galaxy and hid from the Empire to avoid being killed. But they were honorable and loyal. For them, "the way" was a life of sacrificial service. They cared for foundlings and their next generation. While hesitant, Djaran made protecting the Child his mission, even if it meant confronting his people's enemies.

You, too, have been taught how to be like Jesus. Reading this book has been part of that. Now is the time to live it out. Jesus summarized the Christian life by saying, "'Love the Lord your God with all your heart and with all your soul and with all your mind.' This is the first and greatest commandment. And the second is like it: 'Love your neighbor as yourself'" (Matt. 22:37-39).

This is the way.

Quest of the Day

1. Read Isaiah 30.

2. Take 10 minutes or so to journal about a hard thing that you know you need to do, especially if it involves someone else. Could it be standing up for someone who's being bullied? Telling the truth when a lie would help you? Refraining from sexual immorality?

3. Once you've determined what this is, go and do it. This is the way.

DAY 42 - THE UNMATCHED SINBAD
BY ERIC ANDERSON

I know what it is to be in need, and I know what it is to have plenty. I have learned the secret of being content in any and every situation, whether well fed or hungry, whether living in plenty or in want.

Philippians 4:12

Have you read the stories about Sinbad the Sailor? They originated in the collection of short stories known as *1001 Arabian Nights*. Some of his tales inspired some wonderful stop-motion creature features by the one and only Ray Harryhausen. In the written stories Sinbad is an old man recounting his adventures to a young porter named Hinbad, who stops from a hard work for a rest just outside Sinbad's home. The porter sees how lavishly he lives and is overheard by our hero complaining in prayer:

> Almighty Creator of all things, consider the difference between Sindbad and me! I am every day exposed to fatigues and calamities, and can scarcely get coarse barley bread for myself and my family, while happy Sindbad profusely expends immense riches, and leads a life of continual pleasure. What has he done to obtain

from Thee a lot so agreeable? And what have I done to deserve one so wretched?

Sinbad has him brought in to join the party. He tells the porter about his adventures over seven days; one for each day. In this he answers Hinbad's questions with a lot to digest. He starts off by admitting his earliest adult years were not so adventurous or profitable. In fact, he started by going down the same road as a young man—the Prodigal Son—in a story Jesus told in Luke 15. Sinbad shares:

My father was a wealthy merchant of much repute. He bequeathed me a large estate, which I wasted in riotous living. I quickly perceived my error, and that I was misspending my time, which is of all things the most valuable. I remembered the saying of the great Solomon, which I had frequently heard from my father, "A good name is better than precious ointment," and again, "Wisdom is good with an inheritance." Struck with these reflections, I resolved to walk in my father's ways, and I entered into a contract with some merchants, and embarked with them on board a ship we had jointly fitted out.

I should not find it surprising that before sharing his amazing journeys he admits an error in his life and quotes the

Bible. While in the Middle East, I learned that in Arabic culture a belief and trust in God is expected, and it is considered an oddity when someone doesn't believe in God. Sinbad quotes Ecclesiastes 7:1 and 7:11. In Ecclesiastes, Solomon recounts his attempts to understand the meaning of life. Just like the Prodigal Son, Sinbad had been wasting his time in riotous living, but unlike the Prodigal Son, he quickly chose to find something more profitable.

I will admit, I'm not always good with my own time management. Sometimes I have ideas and don't set out to see them come to fruition, and other times I get bogged down with distractions like *Ducktales*...which is at least a quality distraction. Some distraction is good. We need some healthy escapism in life. The problem comes when it becomes all-encompassing to the point that you are not being useful for yourself or those around you. What about the not-so-quality distractions: lust, anger, fear, greed, etc.? These distractions can harm you and others. They affect your outlook on life and your outlook toward other people. No matter the distraction, we must learn to ask ourselves "what one or two useful things can I do today?"

Remember what the Prodigal Son from Jesus's story expected when he decided to turn back and go home? He expected to be a servant. He did not go expecting a warm welcome, but he received one, anyway. His father valued him, and yes, his other son as well, far more than the wealth he had accumulated.

In Genesis 12:2, God told Abraham, "I will make you into a great nation, and I will bless you; I will make your name great, and you will be a blessing." When God sent Abraham on his journey there was no expectation that he would hold all the blessing for himself. Nor are we as Christians to hold it all to ourselves. Sinbad shows this in his own life. Every time he comes back from a voyage, he makes contributions to the poor, and each night sends a bit of wealth home with Hinbad, even the first day they meet. Generosity is an important part of providence, because God expects us to extend the blessings to others.

Sinbad did not want his life to be wasted. Sharing his wealth with others was a big part of that, but not the only piece. Another piece was the adventures themselves. When telling of his third voyage he says, "I soon grew weary of a life of idleness…." While the second voyage had been inspired somewhat by greed, this third voyage was inspired by a desire to go out, explore, and do something useful. Thus we are drawn to a Biblical character who was very zealous to go on voyages for higher purpose: Paul the Apostle to the Gentiles. You see, Sinbad's life is a combination of the Prodigal Son and the former persecutor-turned-apostle for Christ. He started out wasting his life by persecuting the church. Wasting life does not always mean partying. Sometimes it means hurting others and working against what God is doing. That is how Paul wasted his life before coming to Christ on the road to Damascus. But the important thing about Paul was how he used his life after knowing Christ. He traveled on three journeys preaching Christ to those who had not heard of Him. There may well have been more journeys; some scholars think he was imprisoned twice in Rome and possibly went to Spain between the prison sentences for ministry and evangelism.

This life of purpose should come with many warnings. You think your life is hard, just like Hinbad? Voyages are hard, be they merchant voyages or missionary journeys. Paul and Sinbad can tell you about shipwrecks, peril, and difficulty. Sinbad has been left behind and stranded, held captive by a giant cyclops, chased by giant serpents, buried alive with his dead wife, left alone in the open sea and faced more dangers. Paul expressed the hardships he faced for the Gospel in 2 Corinthians 11:24-27.

> "Five times I received from the Jews the forty lashes minus one. Three times I was beaten with rods, once I was pelted with stones, three times I was shipwrecked. I spent a night and a day in the open sea. I have been constantly on the move. I have been in danger from rivers, in danger from bandits, in danger from my fellow

Jews, in danger from Gentiles, in danger in the city, in danger in the country, in danger at sea, in danger form unbelievers. I have labored and toiled I have gone without sleep; I have known hunger and thirst and have gone without food; I have been cold and naked."

Both Paul and Sinbad kept going back on these voyages! With all these terrible things happening to them, they kept going out for more. The purpose and the adventure were so alluring that the pain could not keep them away from it.

Do you have an attitude like peanut butter? Do you stick to anything and persevere through it? Paul handled it with prayer and with thanksgiving for the good providence of God. Paul wrote out several prayers in his letters that are left to us in the New Testament and we have these prayers now to encourage us during our difficulty, whether that is the frustration of a job that seems to be draining us (like Hinbad the Porter), or if we are on an adventure that is frustrating and hard (like Sinbad).

Hinbad wondered how Sinbad had more providence in his life. We have looked at three aspects of his life that were important:

1. A move from wasting time to using it well.

2. An attitude of seeking to bless others.

3. A will to persevere through the hard times.

Ultimately, Paul sought to build a life in service to God. Even when he was persecuting the church, he thought he was serving God. Nothing in Scripture says we will ever get everything we want, but Paul exhibits a life of contentment that includes these traits.

<u>Quest of the Day</u>

1. Read one of the great journeys of the Bible. It could be Abraham, Joseph, Jonah, Paul's missionary journeys, etc.
2. Journal about what you learn.
3. Find someone and tell them a story of how God brought you through difficulty.

ACKNOWLEDGEMENTS

Stop me if you've heard this one: How many people does it take to make a devotional book? The answer: More than you think.

First, we want to thank our team of writers for their contributions! No matter how many entries they wrote, this book wouldn't be what it is without them. Also, thank you for your patience in the editing process!

Next, Ruth Pike-Miller created yet another epic cover for this book, which was arranged by Bryan Donihue for publication.

We had several beta readers who gave us feedback on the book: David Celeskey, Dave Mattingly, Nate Chen, and Gregory Meyer. Thank you!

Eric would like to thank his mom, Vonny Anderson, for sitting with him through a couple movies while he paused and rewound, excessively to get details and quotes right.

A big "thank you" to ministries like the Christian Gamers Guild, GameChurch, Costumers for Christ, and many others who have encouraged us in writing these books. May they be a great resource for you!

And of course, praise Jesus for making us all nerds!
-Eric and Nathan

ABOUT THE AUTHORS

Eric Anderson is a substitute teacher by day and the Quest Commander at Nerd Chapel by night. He has a B.A. in Biblical Studies and Christian Ministries from Taylor University Fort Wayne. His hobbies include reading, board games, swing dancing, and watching television/movies. Read more of his thoughts at www.nerdchapel.com, where you can also learn about the Nerd Chapel schedule, which includes convention appearances, speaking engagements, and tabletop gaming events.

Nathan Marchand hails from Indiana. He attended Taylor University Fort Wayne, earning a B.A. in professional writing, and recently graduated from Purdue University Fort Wayne with an M.A. in English. He's worked as a reporter and a freelance writer, among other things. His first novel, *Pandora's Box*, was published in 2010. He's also the co-creator of the fantasy book series *Children of the Wells* (read more at www.ChildrenoftheWells.com) and the host of the podcast, The Monster Island Film Vault (listen at www.MonsterIslandFilmVault.com). He also enjoys ballroom dancing, photography, acting, and occasionally saving the world. His website is www.NathanJSMarchand.com.

Darrin Ball is a Christian, elder, Bible teacher, husband, and postal worker. He has two more weeks as a husband than working for the postal service (26 years). The Orange Mailman is his appellation as a gamer, blogger, and eschatology buff. He loves Christ, the Bible, his wife, the color orange, peanut butter, games (especially Heroscape), bicycling, comic strips, and LOTR.

Nick Hayden is a writer, a middle-school English teacher, a podcaster, a youth leader, a husband, and a father of three. He enjoys all of these roles. Check out his podcast Derailed Trains of Thought, or visit his inconsistently updated website, www.worksofnick.com.

Chris Cooke is a former social ministry worker, the host/creator/editor of the One Cross Radio Podcast, and occasional devotional writer. You can see more of his works in *Faith and Fandom* Vol 7. Chris has a deep love and passion for people and the Lord, is married to an amazing wife Jill, has an adorable and wonderful puppy Luna, is part of many fandoms, enjoys sharing thoughts about pop culture and faith, and enjoys making videos and music loops for podcasts in Garageband. You can see more at www.onecrossradiopodcast.com.

Becky Smith is a born-again Christian and has been a super fan of anime since the early '90s. She is the host of the Redeemed Otaku Podcast, where she seeks to share the Gospel with her fellow otaku and remind believers that anime is cool, but Jesus is better. She enjoys reading, drawing, and playing video games. She is a full-time wife and crazy cat lady and loves LEGOs, dinosaurs, dragons, and military aircraft. You can listen to her podcast at www.redeemedotaku.libsyn.com.

Mild-mannered minister by day, **Scott Bayles** often spends his weekends in a cape and cowl! He is the co-founder of Costumers for Christ, a non-profit ministry that uses comics and cosplay to share the story of Christ. He's also the award-winning author of *Holy Heroes: The Gospel According to DC & Marvel* and *The Holy Heroes Devotional*, as well as the illustrator of *Jesus Christ: The World's Greatest Hero*. Scott lives with his family in Palmyra, Illinois, where he pastors Blooming Grove Christian Church. You can learn more at www.holyheroes.org.

Made in the USA
Monee, IL
01 October 2025

31211076R00122